GM
6.2
BLA

 Co-published with the International Public Relations Association

INTERNATIONAL PUBLIC RELATIONS

Second Edition

Edited by

SAM BLACK

 POPLOTAN

KOGAN PAGE

5304B
10/97

YOURS TO HAVE AND TO HOLD
BUT NOT TO COPY

First published in 1993

This edition published in 1995

Apart from any fair dealing for the purposes of research or private study, or criticism or review, as permitted under the Copyright, Designs and Patents Act, 1988, this publication may only be reproduced, stored or transmitted, in any form or by any means, with the prior permission in writing of the publishers, or in the case of reprographic reproduction in accordance with the terms and licences issued by the CLA. Enquiries concerning reproduction outside those terms should be sent to the publishers at the undermentioned address:

Kogan Page Limited
120 Pentonville Road
London N1 9JN

© Sam Black 1993, 1995

British Library Cataloguing in Publication Data

A CIP record for this book is available from the British Library

ISBN 0 7494 1756 0

Typeset by BookEns Ltd, Royston, Herts.
Printed and bound in Great Britain by Biddles Ltd,
Guildford and Kings Lynn

INTERNATIONAL
PUBLIC
RELATIONS

Second Edition

'For my wife, Gwen, with sincere thanks for her encouragement and for reading critically all of the first drafts of this book.'

Contents

List of Figures

Foreword

by Betul Mardin, President of the International Public Relations Association

The IPRA Golden World Awards for Excellence were introduced by the Association in 1990 to honour excellence in public relations practice. Somewhat similar schemes have been operating successfully for some years but the new IPRA scheme is unique in its worldwide coverage.

Each year since 1990 over 100 entries have been received from more than 30 different countries and the international jury of judges has had a difficult task selecting the most meritorious cases.

In 1992, through the initiative of the International Foundation for Public Relations Studies, Kogan Page commissioned a casebook of Golden World Award winners, selected primarily for their quality but also for their geographical spread.

That book, *International Public Relations Case Studies*, edited by Professor Sam Black, contained 40 case studies from 15 different countries and was published in 1993. By early 1995, the first edition of the book was sold out and Kogan Page suggested that the second edition should be published quickly in view of the obvious demand.

This new edition again constitutes 40 cases from 15 different countries but a number of new Golden World Award winners from the 1993 and 1994 entries have been selected by the editor to replace some of the older examples in the first edition.

On behalf of the International Public Relations Association, I am very pleased to welcome this new edition and to commend it to students and practitioners who wish to study new methods of meeting the ever expanding demands on our services.

Finally, we wish to thank our original sponsors, the Nissan

Motor Company Limited and our continuing sponsors, the NEC Corporation.

Our thanks are also due to Roy Sanada and to many other IPRA members who have voluntarily devoted much time and energy to ensuring the success of the annual awards, and to the international judges, some of whom have served several years. Special thanks are due to Sam Black who has edited these two editions and who gave the scheme such a good start as chairman of the judges in 1990 and 1991.

April 1995

Preface

This book of case studies includes examples from many different countries and covers many different aspects of public relations practice. It bears out the contention that the theory and philosophy of public relations is the same worldwide. The actual planning and implementation of a public relations programme varies, however, according to the economic, cultural, religious and social character of the country in which it is performed. It has become a truism that public relations can be planned globally but must be carried out locally.

The institution of the annual IPRA Golden World Awards for Excellence in 1990, sponsored by the Nissan Motor Company Ltd, provided an incentive for IPRA members, and others, to look out for programmes of which they were proud and to enter them for competition with case studies from other countries. The result was a wide tapestry of public relations programmes from all over the world. Not surprisingly, the largest number of entries came from the United States and Europe but golden trophies were also won by entries from Kenya, Hungary, China, the Philippines and other countries where the profession is comparatively new.

The 40 case studies selected for this volume come from 15 countries and it is noteworthy that some of the most interesting studies come from small in-house public relations departments or relatively small consultancies.

Each case study has its own particular characteristics but the selected cases emphasise that public relations is a management discipline that has to be planned as a part of the corporate strategy and objectives. Any campaign must be based on valid research, planned carefully and implemented effectively, with meticulous attention to detail; and monitored to ensure that it is meeting its objectives within the appropriate time scale. Finally, the results should be evaluated carefully as even the most supportive management or client will want to know what they are receiving for their provision of finance and resources.

In the studies in this book, the same pattern of presentation has been adopted as was called for in the Golden World Awards. The studies have been divided into background, planning, implementation and evaluation. This is the general pattern which has been followed, but there are some variations where the nature of the report demanded it.

The allocation of individual case studies to particular chapters in the book was somewhat arbitrary and presented difficulties as many cases could be equally appropriately placed in several different chapters. It is hoped that this will not present problems for readers wishing to use the book for reference purposes.

Seldom do circumstances present the same challenges and opportunities, but a careful appraisal of the methods used in these reports from different countries should suggest ways of tackling many situations which can undoubtedly benefit from public relations attention and initiatives.

These case studies relate to work carried out in the last two or three years so a few of the background details may have altered a little. This should not detract from the value of these case studies since our objective is not to tell the reader how to solve any particular problem but rather to explain how good public relations principles and techniques have been used successfully to cope with a wide variety of challenges and opportunities in many different countries. Dr Edward L Bernays, the father of modern professional public relations practice, has defined it as 'an art applied to a science'. These 40 case studies pay tribute to this definition.

We are grateful to the Nissan Motor Company Ltd, now followed by the NEC Corporation, for sponsoring these awards of excellence which have encouraged so many practitioners to match their efforts against those of their peers.

Sam Black
January 1993

Preface to the
Second Edition

The first edition of this casebook was very well received, so much so that supplies of the edition were soon exhausted.

Instead of reprinting, Kogan Page suggested that as the IPRA Golden World Awards for Excellence attract further entries each year, it would be a good idea to bring out a second edition promptly, containing some of the best case studies of more recent years.

This idea was welcomed by the IPRA Board of Directors and this new edition is the result. Kogan Page have suggested that future editions of the casebook should be updated in the same manner.

Sam Black
April 1995

1

Corporate and Business

Case 1.1 Issues management at A T Kearney

BACKGROUND

This is an account of how A T Kearney, a medium-sized management consulting firm with world headquarters in Chicago, Illinois, USA, had a goal of achieving dramatic growth in size and reputation. One of the strategies adopted was for the firm and its individual partners to be recognised as thought leaders on key strategic business issues of the day. Increasing thought leadership was the main objective of the firm's marketing and public relations communications activities, including publications, media relations, seminars and direct mail.

The chairman's vision was the force behind the campaign to study and speak out on the competitiveness of US manufacturing companies. This research effort included surveying manufacturing chief executives, interviewing economists and other experts and profiling nine successful companies. Findings were collected and synthesised in a series of four white papers, an executive magazine supplement, speeches and news publicity articles.

RESEARCH

While A T Kearney was known for its work in a variety of industry and functional areas, it was not well identified with senior management business issues. The firm's lack of standing as management thought leaders became apparent as they researched opinion and planned public relations activities, interviewed public relations agencies and sought placements in the US business media.

Several agencies were engaged to do soft soundings on the firm. In the United States the soundings were done primarily with the news media. In Europe, the soundings also included business executives.

These informal findings confirmed the firm's own experience. They seldom received incoming calls from the news media and were excluded from most round-up stories on important business issues or the management consulting profession.

By the mid-1980s, A T Kearney had evolved into a multi-disciplinary comprehensive firm, but their image was still based in the 1960s. It became obvious that positive action was needed to make executives and the news media think of Kearney as a management consulting firm that deals with strategic issues.

The first step was to review existing research and commentary on competitiveness. Considerable data existed on the subject, but it was almost entirely on the macroeconomic level. It was agreed that Kearney could contribute most to the discourse by focusing on the microeconomic level where their findings would be enhanced by the firm's long tradition of work with manufacturers.

The primary audience for this study was senior business executives, influence leaders in their own right and key consumers of management consulting services. This audience is represented by the 13,000 companies and 45,000 individuals on the mailing list of US companies with more than $100 million in annual revenues.

The secondary audience was writers and editors of key business and financial publications world-wide. Finally, they also wanted to reach senior executives in non-manufacturing industries and in other countries, economists and public officials concerned with foreign trade, commerce and the economy.

PLANNING

The strategy decided upon was to position A T Kearney and its chairman as thought leaders on a very important issue of the day – how US companies can improve their competitive positions against foreign competitors and how they can gain and sustain competitive advantage in the global marketplace. Studying this subject would help the firm to provide added value to clients through increased knowledge of the competitive landscape.

Primary objectives were to improve visibility for Kearney among clients and prospective clients and in the business press and to associate the firm with the most prestigious executives and commentators on the topic of competitiveness.

Secondary objectives were to begin building a public image for the chairman as a business statesman and influence leader and to gain interviews and speaking invitations for him before key business forums.

Success would be measured by the extent of visibility in existing publications and media coverage of the research and publicity of the speaking platforms. No budget was established for the project. The total cost, including design, printing, outside consulting services and the cost of the supplement in the *Chief Executive* magazine, was approximately $175,000, excluding staff costs.

The policy was to view competitiveness from several angles, primarily from the viewpoint of the activities of actual companies, because it was believed that it was companies, not nations, that compete.

EXECUTION

Kearney conducted three phases of primary research:

1. A direct mail survey to which 200 US manufacturing chief executive officers responded on the status and activities of their companies;
2. Interviews with 21 prominent economists and commentators;
3. In-depth interviews resulting in profiles of particularly successful companies.

Comparative data was also used from existing research databases in the firm.

The survey research was conducted by Kearney consultants who wrote preliminary drafts for the first two white papers. An outside author and consultant conducted the interviews and drafted the third white paper. The corporate communications staff wrote the CEO brief, a sponsored supplement for the *Chief Executive* magazine and the fourth white paper. This synthesised the three research projects and presented the firm's agenda for competitive improvement. They also rewrote the first three white papers. Corporate communications was responsible for producing the four white papers, all mailings, publicity, article placements and speech writing. The design of the white papers was done in-house according to corporate identity specifications.

The staff of *Chief Executive* magazine designed and produced the CEO brief. It was sent to the magazine's entire circulation and extra copies were ordered for general circulation. The outside consultant was Dr Leon C Martel, an author and lecturer who is now senior vice-president of research for The Conference Board.

The project was conceived in 1987 with the initial research

conducted at the end of the year and throughout 1988. Three of the four white papers and the CEO brief were published in 1989. Most of the speeches were presented in 1989 or later.

The basic plan was carried out as originally planned. The two Kearney consultants and the corporate communications staff spent 4200 hours on the project over a two-year period. The decision to sponsor the CEO brief was made later when the magazine proposed that Kearney be invited to be the first sponsor of its new supplement series.

During the course of the project, there was fine tuning of the framework in which the material was presented and the way collateral issues were articulated. This was unavoidable because the topic of competitiveness was a moving target as political and economic events brought new issues to light or changed the focus of existing issues.

The four white papers were mailed consecutively to 5000 senior executives of manufacturing companies in the United States.

EVALUATION

The primary goal — increased thought leadership for the firm among senior executive consumers of management consulting — is an ongoing effort. The firm, however, doubled in size since the study was initiated and part of the credit was attributed to the communications efforts. Other immediate results include the following:

- Since 1989, the chairman of Kearney has given numerous speeches, including The International Industrial Conference, the American Chamber of Commerce in Japan, the UCLA Anderson School of Business, the Spheres of Influence Forum sponsored by the Premier of Ontario, Canada, as well as at a round table sponsored by *Directors and Boards* magazine. His growing visibility as a thought leader has led to appointments to the boards of directors of The Conference Board, The National Association of Manufacturers and Maytag Corporation.
- The chairman received letters from 35 senior executives congratulating the firm on the stance they had taken on the issue. Requests were received for an additional 3000 copies of each of the three white papers.
- Initial media news coverage of the manufacturing survey included a syndicated Tom Peters column and reports in *Industry Week, Business Month, Business Marketing* and *Financial News Network*. In Germany, *Industriemagazin* published a four-

part article. The study was released in Japan and received good coverage in the print and television media.

- The chairman gave in-depth interviews in several European countries. He also wrote articles for *Institutional Investor, Business Horizons, Directors and Boards* and several other publications. Many other authors have referred to the study in their own writings, including an article in *Harvard Business Review*.

- This study was the start of a major media relations programme for A T Kearney. As the firm gained more visibility in the media during the first two years, more opportunities were found for a wide coverage of the findings. The most gratifying result was that on average 50 incoming calls a month were received from the news media in the United States alone, and Kearney consultants were quoted in 1130 articles in 1990. Prior to this programme being initiated, fewer than five calls a month were received from the news throughout the world.

- The supplement in *Chief Executive* was highly successful and has become a regular feature for them. Kearney sponsored a second supplement in 1992 on globalism.

- The corporate communications staff at the firm's headquarters has been increased to 13 since the beginning of the competitiveness programme. The firm has also retained eight public relations agencies in seven countries. Senior management's commitment to thought leadership continues to strengthen with each success.

CASE DISCUSSION

This is an example of a fairly new phenomenon in which consultants of different specialties have turned to public relations to increase their reputation and their practices or businesses. This is not so new in the United States but in many countries, such as the United Kingdom, it is only recently that professions have been permitted to advertise and use promotional activities like public relations.

The methods used to promote a firm of management consultants such as A T Kearney of Chicago will, naturally, be quite different from those applicable to a large manufacturing company or other profit-seeking businesses. The reputation of a firm of consultants is the sum total of the reputation of the senior partners and the efficiency of their organisation. This was realised clearly by the senior management of A T Kearney who decided on a positive programme to enhance the reputation of their company through the statements of their chairman and the white papers published. They wisely selected one important issue — how US companies could improve their competitive advantage. Having decided to make this the focus of their programme, they researched the subject very carefully before they embarked on the production of the four white papers.

A well-known company of management consultants in the UK had a similar desire to promote their group which had a fine tradition but was not so well known as previously. Enquiry revealed that the senior partners had published a number of excellent monographs on various management subjects. On inspection, it was surprising to find that these excellent books, which were all published by the company, displayed no family resemblance. They were quite different in format and cover design and no book made any reference to the company or to the other books. This mistake was not made by Kearney. Each white paper was clearly part of a series and the back cover described the company and its major activities.

This type of public relations through the publication of books or articles is very effective provided the content of the publications is accurate, informative and worth publishing in its own right. If not, any immediate benefit may well be counteracted by subsequent exposure.

Case 1.2 Introducing 'Parcelforce'

BACKGROUND

The British Post Office has seen many changes since 1986 both in structure and the manner in which it operates. The old Post Office has become the Post Office Group, structured like a public group of companies with its holding company, the Post Office Corporation. The three main subsidiaries are the Royal Mail (letters), Parcelforce and Post Office Counters Ltd, the over-the-counter service. Giro-bank, the bank that was part of the Post Office, was sold in 1990.

The Post Office group operates on an efficient, profitable and commercial footing as a private sector company, yet has a social role which few businesses would accept. For example, Royal Mail delivers letters to all of the UK (no matter how remote) at a uniform cost and Post Office Counters Ltd retains a large proportion of unprofitable outlets in rural areas.

Royal Mail remains the only legal pay-as-you-use system of mail between members of the public. There are, however, many private companies who provide business mail services, such as the system used by the legal profession and building societies, on a subscription basis.

Royal Mail Parcels had a particular need to be more efficient because it was the only Post Office division operating in a free market and had to compete with the phenomenal growth of the independent parcels companies in the 1970s following deregulation of the parcel-delivery services. The growth in demand for faster and more frequent delivery of goods can be seen to reflect the move by many businesses towards operations based on the principle of 'just in time' management – ie the reduction of stock-holding and a reliance on the more frequent supply of components, raw materials and other stocks by suppliers. Parcel delivery companies were forced to become much more sensitive to the demands of customers who needed guaranteed time deliveries, which gave rise to the introduction of express delivery and courier services.

There were also other factors which contributed to the development of a more competitive parcels delivery market: road transport systems were improving nationally within the UK.

The reputation of the Post Office parcel deliveries service suffered as a result of the first postal strike in 1971. The postal service's reputation for reliability suffered further damage during the 1970s due to the problems encountered with its main carrier, British Rail.

The 1980s saw further development of the express delivery market when large international companies such as DHL, TNT, Securicor and Federal Express developed high marketing profiles.

From 1986, the new Royal Mail Parcels management refocused marketing and invested in better services, meeting the demands of business customers in the highly lucrative distribution business. In three years they developed new networks, more sophisticated technology, additional products, an expanding vehicle fleet, and a dedicated salesforce. In 1987, a customer care communication campaign started, establishing in a year 19 customer care units linked to an enquiry centre, to confront, and be seen to confront, the reliability of the service directly with the customer.

In 1988 £30 million was invested to:

- develop a 'Super Service' based on 11 regional centres and 75 satellite depots as an independent network which offered guaranteed 24-hour or 48-hour delivery;
- improve the already established *Datapost*, the express service for goods and documents;
- gear-up international services for the expected expansion in European traffic after 1993 including Datapost EMS (Express Mail Services);
- introduce a tracking service, 'Trakbak', which confirmed delivery of the standard parcel service using a bar-code system which was linked to an enquiry centre.

In 1989 £35 million was invested in new vehicles. By 1990, Royal Mail Parcels was a clear market leader in the £1.5 million domestic parcels market, with a 30 per cent share. Competitors were still the international carriers and courier firms. Ninety five per cent of users of the Post Office parcels services were business customers.

Plans to create a new visual identity for Royal Mail Parcels began alongside this reorganisation of services. As the service developed, corporate identity consultants Newell and Sorrell developed the new look and new name (see Figure 1), researching customers and employees at regular intervals about their view of the business and having periodic discussions with key figures in the industry about their opinion of the way forward.

Figure 1 The new Parcelforce logo

RESEARCH

The principal issue of concern in a public relations context was the corporate image: why the popular image was out of date and did not fit the actual business; why it needed to change in name and appearance and what the change could achieve for the business and the Post Office. There were several marketing messages to be conveyed and the possibility of a hidden agenda to be confronted.

The issues of privatisation and future global competition were 'hidden agendas' because each depended on political outcomes in Britain and Europe rather than the events in hand. While they were not within the control of the public relations remit, they were issues that would inevitably have to be dealt with by Parcelforce spokespersons.

During their research for the development of a new corporate identity, the consultants found that the customers' image of the Royal Mail's parcels service was non-existent or else that it existed as part of the Post Office – a 'brown paper parcel and string' image. Although Royal Mail Parcels had by far the highest number of collection and delivery points (post offices and van depots), other companies in the private sector were better known as parcel services.

Royal Mail Parcels were thus leaders in the market without projecting themselves as such. In other words the corporate image of a small public sector service for customers did not match the reality of its lead position in a business sector market. The public sector label clearly did not evoke the image of a competitive business. The prominent image of the other services in the parcels market, created and reinforced by advertising, probably contributed to this.

NEED FOR CHANGE

The forceful marketing and advertising employed by the main private sector competitors had earned them go-getting images with which to woo customers and gradually eat into Royal Mail Parcels' market share. Much was at stake, with a market growing at ten per cent a year, particularly in the express sector. Researchers estimated that the world market for all air cargo was worth £11 billion, forecast to grow to £35 billion by 1995, of which no less than 70 per cent will be express traffic. A particular threat was the impending introduction of a new service in Britain by the American giant USP.

Thus by February 1990, Royal Mail Parcels was ready to be reborn as a new company, *Parcelforce*, with a more positive identity that would differentiate its products. By changing the visual image and name of Royal Mail Parcels, the product and service would be associated in the minds of businessmen as a new, improved service and not the old Royal Mail one. While the old Royal Mail could conceivably have changed its image through its service alone, the process would have taken longer without the attention-drawing value of a new visual identity. The projection of the new image acted as a catalyst for the perception of a cultural change in the organisation.

At the same time, there was no desire to divorce the division totally from Royal Mail because of its tradition in social responsibility. Research showed that there was great public and employee loyalty to the Post Office and Royal Mail. The identity consultants retained the Royal Mail name and crest (in gold rather than yellow) above the large Parcelforce logo. The base background colour for the vans was still pillarbox red, thus retaining the Post Office heritage.

SIGNIFICANCE OF THE NEW IDENTITY

The birth of Parcelforce marked the final separation of operations from Royal Mail Letters and the announcement of more than £80 million to establish its own 150 local collection and delivery depots in the next three years. Within that time the size of the fleet of vehicles would be nearly doubled to 10,000 and 5000 employees would be taken on. Computerisation of national centres and bar coding would be the investments for reliability. In Britain they would be offering the most powerful network for parcels completely independent from Royal Mail.

The perception of the changed image reflected exactly the change that had happened in the business. Parcelforce had evolved as an independent, more dynamic organisation able to compete in a sensitive market. The diamond-shaped part of the Parcelforce logo symbolised the company as a 'jewel' (in the crown) of the Royal Mail service, yet it still offered the social responsibility of Royal Mail and the goodwill from Post Office Counters.

ANNOUNCING THE CHANGE

A £3 million advertising campaign and direct mail shots to 200,000 British companies also supported the launch of the identity change. Consultants Ogilvy & Mather in London provided direct marketing services and conducted a public relations campaign to rectify the image problem and work towards the launch of the Parcelforce corporate identity and the investment announcement.

PLANNING

The role of public relations was to complement and reinforce the work done by the specialist consultants on changing the corporate identity. They had to promote a modern image to the business community while keeping the public's loyalty to a traditional service.

The consultants decided that to launch Parcelforce as a major power in the distribution market, they had to convey the position of Parcelforce as the leading distribution company in the UK; one that is innovative, dynamic and efficient. In other words, their goal was to increase awareness and usage of Parcelforce. A measurable goal would be media response to the new identity and the number and nature of business contracts gained after the launch.

To create awareness, they decided to saturate the media with information before, during and after the launch. Different angles to the Parcelforce story targeted at different types of media would avoid journalistic staleness. To ensure producing the right sort of information for the media, Ogilvy & Mather conducted a survey to gain the media's perception of Royal Mail Parcels and its services before it became Parcelforce.

Their findings showed there was an extremely low level of awareness and that journalists were highly critical. Many had not received information from the company. Many did not know about the market competitiveness of Royal Mail Parcels and leading journalists still had the image of 'grannies' parcels' only being handled by Royal Mail Parcels.

The consultants sought to increase usage of Parcelforce through creating awareness among indirect target audiences – the national, regional and specialist press. They deduced that media publicity would reinforce the awareness built up by pre-launch marketing activities. The consultancy decided on an 'education process' for the media so that journalists could portray the idea of the new identity in an informative and positive way. The educational activities included:

1. Design and production of an information pack of fact sheets covering the background to Parcelforce, the three-year investment programme in the past and the future, the market information, the three-year corporate identity programme and its relevance to the market.
2. Media briefings on the distribution industry with national and business press.
3. Exhibition stands at relevant exhibitions.
4. Sponsorship activities to reinforce the Parcelforce name.
5. Production of a photo library to satisfy future media requests.

To ensure that the media would get the best and most informative response at the time of the national launch, Parcelforce wanted to develop a network of public relations representatives in each of their regions around the UK. The consultants took on a teaching role and orchestrated a seminar for all the Parcelforce representatives on the role of public relations. These seminars were run throughout 1989 to prepare the regional representatives for the launch in February 1990. Seminars were always supported by public relations manuals and guidance notes, because the consultants thought it important to project the same message to the business community and all other consumers during the launch. For all the key spokespersons at national and regional level, the consultancy provided media training programmes so that they could become familiar with print and broadcast media techniques.

The main launch event was a news conference in the Grosvenor House Hotel, London, with guest speeches and a multi-projection AV slide presentation. Live TV and radio link-ups were arranged around the country. The slide presentation subsequently toured around the UK in a regional roadshow for business customers, travelling to 12 venues for three weeks and covering England, Scotland, Wales and Ireland. The consultancy organised and briefed Parcelforce spokespersons around the country on how to give interviews and set up photographic opportunities in each region showing vans, motor bikes and lorries with the new liveries for Parcelforce.

In case broadcast journalists did not have access to live material, the consultancy syndicated audio and visual news releases for radio and TV stations through agencies. For the print media, they provided press releases, captioned photos, PMTs (photosensitive versions of logos to be used in printing), newly-designed Parcelforce brochures and fact sheets. A national press and TV advertising campaign was run along with the media relations campaign in the week of the launch to gain maximum exposure of the new name.

The 'inside story' of splitting up the Post Office into saleable assets in advance of privatisation had been brewing ever since the three trading divisions became separately managed. During periods of industrial disruption, or whenever the price of stamps went up, media articles speculated on privatisation. The public relations campaign did not allude to the privatisation controversy at all in their media information packs, but ensured that Parcelforce spokespersons were adamant about their marketing rationale behind the reorganisation and denied a political rationale.

Saturation of media was achieved. Immediately after the launch of the new corporate identity, positive media coverage burst forth in all the national and regional newspapers. Media coverage in the national, regional, specialist and business press continued in a steady stream for a few months, many of them doing special features on the competition in the parcels market. Several reports pointed out that investing £80 million in the future service made it look like less efficient use of total Royal Mail resources. Many analysed the investment and the sharpening up of management to stimulate more parcels business as a preparation for making Parcelforce an attractive proposition for privatisation.

Coverage was intense, not just because of the media relations campaign, but also because the news value was high: it was a story about the economy (injecting growth in the public sector), political (the privatisation issue), a national institution (with a Royal connection!), of business interest (public-sector borrowing, private-sector marketing, techniques) and contained new information (the parcels market potential). It had targeted both public and business interests.

The consultancy had facilitated long-term media coverage by building up local media relations and continued to win coverage some time after the Parcelforce launch. There was more subsequent media contact directly with Parcelforce. The consultancy also measured the business community profile afterwards. They found it had been raised considerably and contracts were won from competitors.

CASE DISCUSSION

The change of name and the introduction of a new corporate identity were powerful support for the new trading and marketing policies of the organisation. By achieving wide media coverage of Parcelforce's new persona, public relations played its part in the transformation of the organisation from an old-fashioned but reliable way of sending parcels to a new modern delivery service which could compete effectively with all the courier services which have been enjoying so much success.

Corporate identity programmes are a very important part of public relations but they must be an integrated part of an organisation's corporate strategy and not an end in themselves. The Post Office has long enjoyed an excellent reputation for its attention to good industrial design and the way in which graphics have helped to launch Parcelforce have continued this tradition.

It is difficult to measure the effect of the public relations campaign in this launching of Parcelforce because there was also a large direct mail and advertising campaign running simultaneously. It is certain, however, that the very wide media response will have a continuing and cumulative effect.

Case 1.3 Demystifying Technology to win Competitive Advantage

BACKGROUND

As part of the reorganisation of Telstra, Australia's largest telecommunications company, the company created a Network Technology Group (NTG) which would be responsible for its multi-billion dollar investment in research, planning, construction and the operation of its telecommunications network infrastructure and systems.

During 1993–94 the Network Technology Group faced a series of challenges.

1. It was required to undertake a fundamental restructuring of the way in which it did business – by changing work practices, suppliers, operational procedures – with significant impact on numbers of staff and investment in the Australian economy.
2. NTG, while managing this restructure, also had to manage investments of A$2 billion a year, directed towards ensuring that Australians could reap the benefits of the current telecommunications revolution.
3. Simultaneously, Telstra itself was involved in a series of ballots which would determine Telstra's market share and which also required NTG to make a significant contribution to the success of the marketing effort involved.
4. Staff interviews, market research, corporate image monitoring and media content analysis indicated that:
   i)   staff had low morale;
   ii) customers believed that Telstra was a technological laggard rather than a leader and that its competitor was providing better technology;
   iii) media coverage of Telstra technology issues was often negative and controversial;
   iv) the economic value of the NTG programme provided was poorly understood and not appreciated by opinion leaders and the public.
5. While sections of the organisation had had external communication

programmes, the group as a whole had no public relations structure or public relations activity.

The problems and opportunities

The obvious need, given this situation, was to produce a coordinated public relations programme which addressed the disparate issues while creating a competitive corporate image for the new group with its various stakeholders.

RESEARCH

The research methods used to plan the programme and to measure its success were:

1. An analysis of overall Telstra corporate image monitoring material to determine attitudes to the company and its technological positioning.
2. Cumulative monthly media content analysis of all Australian media and all Australian coverage of telecommunication technology to ascertain the tone and value of the coverage.
3. Staff surveys of attitudes towards change and management.
4. Qualitative surveys of staff and customers.

The results of this research indicated that NTG needed to:

- help people understand technology by explaining its role in people's everyday lives;
- reduce ill-informed negative media publicity about its technological performance and to involve staff in the change process.

PLANNING

Objectives

The three main objectives were agreed as:

1. To position NTG as the quality Australian provider of customer-driven, advanced telecommunication technology to Australian communities and Australians wherever they live and work.
2. To help develop a common sense of identity and purpose throughout the NTG staff.

3. To reduce negative publicity about NTG's technological performance and to counteract mistaken market perceptions that the company's main competitor is a technological leader.

Target publics

The *internal* publics were identified as:

- NTG customers (retail units within Telstra) − consumer, commercial, corporate and government;
- NTG staff and their families;
- senior Telecom management.

The *external* publics were:

- the media;
- Telstra customers;
- opinion leaders;
- state ministers, shadow ministers and MPs;
- local government;
- federal MPs;
- suppliers;
- industry bodies;
- community groups.

Strategies

The strategies adopted were:

1. To assemble a multi-disciplinary communication team able to meet the objectives.
2. To undertake a proactive media campaign progressively unveiling the NTG operational and supplier charges while simultaneously reaching key opinion leaders through personal briefings.
3. To focus on the ubiquity of the network, what it makes possible for customers today and tomorrow, and how it provides the fundamental platform on which all Australian telecommunication customer benefits are based.
4. To put a human face on network technology by involving staff in demonstrating the technology to local communities, thereby tapping into the staff's enthusiasm as advocates for the company.
5. To ensure that all communications contributed to raising awareness of the national technological, social and economic benefits which flowed from NTG's activities.

6. To make sure that all the staff understood the essential reasons for change instead of merely being confronted with change.

The messages

The themes adopted were:

- NTG provides the network which makes it possible for all Australians, wherever they live or work, to communicate by voice and data to anyone elsewhere in the world.
- NTG technological initiatives:
  — reduce the cost of telecommunication services;
  — continually improve the quality of the service network for the benefit of customers; and
  — meet new customer needs with a wide range of new services.
- NTG staff are highly motivated telecommunication experts. They built the network, they know the network and they run the network for you.
- NTG investment of A$2 billion a year on infrastructure.
- Telstra's world-class network is essential to Australia being internationally competitive.
- The nature of the telecommunications business is changing and it is necessary to change to stay in it.

The strategy

The key techniques adopted were:

1. To develop an annual programme of major media announcements about new contracts, changes in modes of operation and new technologies; also to provide an overall framework for the programme and to reach the general public, customers and opinion leaders.
2. To undertake a systematic, managed speech, customer contact and briefing programme by senior managers to reach key opinion leaders and stakeholders.
3. To open up the previously fortress-like Telecom local exchanges so that NTG staff could show local communities how the technology which provides their telecommunications services actually works and thus generate positive publicity in local and regional media.
4. To promote a company-wide one-voice approach to technology by keeping corporate and NTG customer units informed

about activities and encouraging them to use key themes in their marketing and communication activities.

5. To conduct a staff communications programme to facilitate change and to win support for external activities.

Management involvement

There was continuing liaison with management, with frequent briefings and regular meetings to plan close collaboration.

IMPLEMENTATION

Media activity

Major media announcements and briefing programmes were undertaken on the following topics:

1. A A$3.3 billion programme to modernise the telecommunication network known as changes in Future Mode of Operation (FMO) designed to bring the benefits of twenty-first century communications to all Australians over a five-year programme.
2. The re-engineering of the network involving staffing and operational changes, an annual report on industry developments which detailed Telstra's total annual budget of A$3 billion investment in Australia, and the precise areas to benefit from it.
3. A series of technological developments such as pay-TV, interactive multi-media services and major contracts.

Following each news release, localised versions designed for all states and regions were developed and distributed.

In particular, technology stories indicating the region-by-region breakdown of FMO investment were localised for areas undergoing ballots and these were used to demonstrate Telecom's investments in specific communities as a means of encouraging customers to choose Telecom.

Briefings and personal contact

All media launches were followed up by personal briefings for federal and state ministers, shadow ministers, officials, backbench MPs and unions.

Senior executives undertook a planned speech programme for addressing appropriate organisations. In total, the NTG group managing director and his network colleagues made 48 major speeches during the year.

A series of small lunches with key customers was organised to help identify their telecommunications needs and to introduce a 'customer culture' to NTG.

Exchange open days

NTG fostered and encouraged the opening of local telephone exchanges to the public in more than 100 metropolitan, suburban and country locations throughout Australia. The exchanges are the initial entry point for customers to the national and global telecommunications network and are usually not open to visitors for security reasons.

These open days were organised by volunteer staff members who demonstrated how the exchanges worked. Before each open day, local advertising and media publicity were used to raise awareness of the open day. Families of Telstra staff and VIPs were invited and other Telstra business units were encouraged to invite their local customers.

The actual open days were used to generate further publicity. Simple displays were used to illustrate NTG activities but the emphasis was on demystifying the technology and linking it to the customer-friendly approach of the local staff. Posters, sample bags and sausage sizzles were provided.

Internal communications

Information activities to keep the staff informed included:

- personal visits by the group managing director to all staff to explain the context for change and to provide staff with an opportunity to raise issues of concern to them;
- staff involvement in open days;
- extension of team-briefing programmes;
- creation of a regular staff newsletter *Telecom Network News*;
- involvement of senior management in staff briefings and motivation programmes.

Issues management

While the programme was taking place, project staff maintained ongoing monitoring of all relevant issues and an issues map which identified possible sources of negative publicity. In each case, proactive strategies were put in place to pre-empt possible negative publicity.

It was also important to develop issues management strategies for each major announcement. All the announcements, while providing national investment benefits, also had profound impact on individual states, suppliers and other stakeholders. It was necessary to carry out extensive pre-briefing sessions to win stakeholder support.

The communications team

An important element in the programme was the recognition that such a major programme required a multi-disciplinary team with a wide range of skills and experience. This created a productive partnership between NTG public relations staff and its consultants, Turnbull Fox Phillips, who worked jointly to develop and implement the agreed strategies. Brian Donovan and Noel Turnbull have produced this report on the programme.

EVALUATION

Media content analysis

1. **Volume**
    The results of the media campaign were measured by detailed content analysis. In the period from April 1993 to June 1994, independent content analysis by Wallis Consulting showed that:
    i)   The number of items concerning NTG issues increased from 123 items per month to 243 items per month – a 97.5 per cent increase.
    ii) While NTG's average volume contribution to total Telecom media coverage over the 12-month period was 20 per cent each month, this figure varied from 11 per cent in January 1993 to 27 per cent in November 1993, to 24 per cent in March 1994 and 33 per cent in April 1994.
    iii) The average net volume of NTG's contribution to Telecom's total media coverage saw a steady increase, with an average 236 items per month for the last six months of 1994.
2. **Tone**
    NTG also increased its proportion of Telecom's positive media coverage and decreased its proportion of Telecom's total negative media coverage.

i) In the 12 months, NTG contributed 20 per cent of Telecom's total positive media tone and 21 per cent of Telecom's total neutral/balanced media tone.

ii) NTG's percentage of total Telecom negative coverage decreased, ranging between 39 and 14 per cent in 1993 down to 6–18 per cent in 1994.

Technology positioning

1. **Community responses**

   More than 40,000 people attended the exchange open days. Forms were provided for attendees to record their reactions. Typical comments were: 'Amazed – didn't realise what was inside an exchange and how technical it all was'; 'Great, very informative'; 'Friendly staff'; 'Does more for Telecom than expensive television and newspaper adverts'; 'Wonderful'; 'We take a lot for granted, don't we?'

2. **Staff feedback**

   Typical staff feedback comments were: 'Made me feel appreciated'; 'I really enjoyed the day and showing visitors what my job entails.' Staff feedback made it clear that the programme motivated staff and gave them a strong sense of involvement.

Corporate image monitor

The latest Telstra corporate image monitor shows that Telecom is considered to be performing at 'very good to excellent' levels on most performance measures, but that its *best* performance is in the areas of 'technical excellence' and 'help to the economy'.

Staff involvement

An independent staff survey showed that in the first six months of 1994 NTG staff recorded:

● a 13.3 per cent increase in favourable views of staff communication;

● a 9 per cent increase in positive identification with the company.

Summary

On the basis of the benchmarks initially used to identify programme needs and the objectives to be achieved, significant positive results were achieved by the campaign.

CASE DISCUSSION

This is a very comprehensive account of a programme to support the introduction of major changes at a very large Australian telecommunications organisation. Coincidentally, the company wished to gain support for its vast expansion programme by explaining the new technologies which bring both problems and opportunities.

The approach was very systematic and logical. A strong communications team was formed, research was carried out to identify the issues which had to be addressed and the objectives were agreed. Internal and external target audiences were classified and suitable themes for the campaign were established.

Communication programmes of this kind require full cooperation from top management and this was obviously forthcoming in this case. The strong support undoubtedly contributed to the successful results.

The independent media analysis produced figures which clearly confirmed the success of the media relations part of the campaign. It will be interesting to learn if these improved media results are maintained in future years.

Case 1.4 Establishing AT&T's identity in Mexico

BACKGROUND

American Telephone & Telegraph (AT&T) began in 1989 with fewer than a dozen people employed in Mexico, most of them United States citizens. The company's only business in that country was providing long-distance service from the United States, in partnership with the Mexican telephone company which received the calls and initiated those from Mexico. Long-distance service was AT&T's traditional business and it was done silently and invisibly, allowing the local company to be out front.

Within two years, AT&T employed more than 1500 workers, most of them Mexicans. The company was inaugurating its third state-of-the-art Mexican factory, and Mexican distributors existed for every major AT&T product and business unit. Further, long-distance opportunities were being aggressively pursued. AT&T was standing prominently at the side of the Mexican telephone company, Telmex.

OBJECTIVES

The overall public relations activities which the company wished to promote during 1990 were:

- to establish the AT&T brand in Mexico using the probable incorporation of AT&T in Mexico as a focal point, and to ensure consistent brand management within markets and coordinated brand management across markets;
- to establish AT&T's identity in Mexico as an industry leader who could solve Mexico's telecommunications problems at all levels of user sophistication, with high quality, highly reliable products and services and integrated solutions;
- to use AT&T Bell Laboratories in order to establish AT&T's experience with technological innovation;
- to stimulate the sale of products and services by working with the business units to provide targeted sales and trade show support, product and services publicity.

To achieve these objectives, the following three-tier approach to public relations activities was recommended:

1. To establish brand awareness, a media programme to be formulated to introduce AT&T de Mexico and development of an AT&T corporate image. This would involve the adoption and consistent use of a common corporate identity signature in all external communications, and also coordination of all local advertising to ensure that it properly and consistently supported mutually agreed AT&T identity. In addition it would involve development and public relations support for the country manager.
2. The development of a basic public relations infrastructure. This would include identifying and training spokespersons, evaluating local media and establishing definitive media lists; establishing press clipping procedures; developing generic country written material; identifying and interviewing local agencies to determine potential for local in-country support; maintaining and updating components for press kits.
3. To support business unit sales imperatives by developing sales support plans for new product and services introduction; for the opening of new facilities; and for periodic update events and media relations at AT&T special presence sites such as microelectronics at Matamoros and consumer products at Guadalajara.

RESEARCH

In order to have an accurate basis on which to plan future public relations activities for AT&T in Mexico, a number of research activities were undertaken. A review of the major Mexican daily newspapers revealed no mention of AT&T in articles about telecommunications and none were recollected by Mexicans queried. A research into the media was conducted and a detailed media list was prepared. Research was conducted into the Mexican telecommunications infrastructure and the opportunities created by privatisation. A statement was prepared on AT&T policies and corporate stance on privatisation. Mexico City and Guadalajara were visited to assess the overall situation and to conduct research by interviewing US government officials, multinational company executives and AT&T directors.

AT&T business needs were researched by interviewing the head of each of AT&T's businesses operating in Mexico: the country manager, International Communication Services, Network Systems, General Business Systems, Consumer Products, Business Communication Systems, Computer Systems, along with the plant managers.

PLANNING

It was agreed that the focal point for AT&T's branding efforts in Mexico should be the incorporation of AT&T de Mexico. This should provide an ideal launching pad from which to establish the common corporate signature – AT&T de Mexico – and to identify the business units which will, under this signature, provide integrated telecommunications solutions for all levels of user sophistication in Mexico.

Following the introduction of AT&T de Mexico, effective management of the AT&T brand in Mexico would require the adoption and consistent use of a common business signature by all business units in their external communications, coordinated and complemented advertising approaches geared towards supporting the agreed upon AT&T identity, and a continual media relations campaign to strengthen public perception of AT&T de Mexico.

The specific recommendations in connection with the launching of AT&T de Mexico were as follows:

1. A press event with key media leaders to announce incorporation, identify business leadership, demonstrate product lines and underscore business units working together to bring integrated solutions to customers. In addition, to arrange complementary press visits for key media.
2. The press event could be a single event or could serve as one event within the context of other positioning events for key government, customer and business leaders.
3. Development of AT&T de Mexico collateral material, along with a strategy for its use with customers.
4. Identification of key media and individuals and the development of a public relations plan to support the building of a working relationship with reporters and editors of all the leading Mexican newspapers.
5. The preparation of an overall image advertising campaign, into which AT&T's distributors can fit their own messages.

Thematically, all material should emphasise AT&T's multi-dimensional unity, historical leadership in telecommunications, and future capabilities as witnessed through AT&T Bell Laboratories, as well as individual products and services.

EVALUATION

It is difficult to evaluate the results in detail as, once launched, the public relations programme gathered momentum and is widening its scope and ramifications. The following comments, however, chronicle some of the early results.

- Newspaper, magazine and television reports have regularly affirmed AT&T's commitment to Mexico.
- The media have associated AT&T with forward-looking technology, which can be used in a partnership with Mexico to solve its telecommunication problems.
- After years of no presence and nil identity in Mexico, AT&T has become a significant player.
- The local telephone company was able to award AT&T the largest share of a network bid, where the political climate and feeling within Telmex would not previously have permitted this. Not only did AT&T receive the $130 million contract, but also won its first switch bid ever in Mexico.
- The long-distance part of AT&T's business, which deals directly with Telmex, has been able to be much more aggressive in offering new services: previously the relationship allowed little give and take.
- AT&T is described more and more in friendly terms, no longer in negative, 'foreign' words. There has not been a negative article about AT&T in the Mexican press since August 1989, shortly before AT&T organised public relations activity in Mexico.

CASE DISCUSSION

There are many morals to be drawn from this case study. Relationships between the United States and Mexico have not always been very friendly. Mexico has long been very suspicious of the intentions of its large neighbour. Having decided to enter the Mexican market on a much larger scale, and using its own name and brand image, AT&T used public relations on a grand scale to prepare the ground for its expanded activities and provided the necessary resources.

AT&T, like other large telecommunications companies, believe in the efficacy of public relations in support of their commercial operations. To achieve such a remarkable effect on Mexican perceptions in such a short time is a tribute both to the value of public relations in such circumstances and the effective manner in which AT&T public relations carried out its brief.

2

Public Affairs

Case 2.1 Combating environmental restraints in Canada

In these days of concern with environmental factors, an attempt to drill for oil off Canada's shores was bound to arouse strong opposition from many directions, particularly from the local fishermen who constituted a strong lobby.

About two years earlier, Texaco Canada had announced an ambitious programme of oil exploration but had failed to secure planning permission to drill. LASMO plc, a smaller oil company, decided to try its luck and started by taking advice from a local public relations company.

BACKGROUND

In mid-1989, LASMO plc, an international oil company with a head office in London, in partnership with a Crown corporation of the Province of Nova Scotia, agreed to pursue development of two off-shore oil deposits, Cohasset and Panuke, located about 250 km south-east of Halifax, Nova Scotia.

It was a very bold decision for only a few months earlier, the *Exxon Valdez* had run aground off Alaska with catastrophic results and so public opinion was fully alerted to the potential dangers of offshore oil operations. Moreover, 15 months earlier the governments of Nova Scotia and Canada had agreed to a moratorium on drilling on George's Bank, located less than 500 nautical km from the Cohasset and Panuke fields, thwarting the ambitious exploration programme planned by Texaco Canada. Figure 2 is a typical news report illustrating the media opposition to Texaco Canada's proposals.

A local public relations company, McArthur, Thompson & Law

THE CHRONICLE~HERALD

Thursday, July 30, 1987

Texaco 'happy' fishermen united in drilling dispute

By BRIAN MEDEL
and JUDY MYRDEN

Texaco Canada Resources intends to meet with a new association of fisherman opposed to drilling on Georges Banks, said Laurie Taylor, Texaco Canada spokesman, on Wednesday.

"We're certainly happy that the fishermen in that area are now united as a group and will address the real issues and concerns and prepare a unified policy. In the past fishermen tended to be fragmented," said Mr. Taylor.

During a closed door meeting Tuesday, a group of Nova Scotia fishing industry representatives united, retained legal counsel and affixed the title 'NORIG' to a contingent of spokesmen as it prepares for the battle of Georges Bank.

Mr. Taylor said the company would like to meet the group as soon as it identifies its concerns and establishes a directorship.

Texaco has established information centres in Barrington Passage and Yarmouth in an effort to reach the fishermen's concerns, he said.

The group, NORIG, fears exploratory drilling on the bank may be imminent and the likelihood of testing is one reason it has quickly forged ahead.

NORIG's lawyer, Ken MacInnis of Halifax, will travel to Gloucester, Mass. today where he and Emily Bateson, program director with the Conservation Law Foundation of New England, will meet with a group of lobster fishermen's wives who were engaged in similar battles.

Ms Bateson, who also attended the founding meeting, said: "We're not an irrational and emotional organization," she said, but emphasized the fact that Georges Bank is extremely vulnerable to damage from oil exploration.

Ms Bateson said any drilling operation would make intentional, daily discharges of ballast water, cuttings from the drill work and sanitary discharges.

She said no oil cleanup equipment can operate if waves exceed six feet but on Georges Bank, waves are often in that range.

Figure 2 Example of the strong press opposition to Texaco Canada's proposals

was retained to work with LASMO Nova Scotia Limited to consider ways of building a better rapprochement with target audiences and thus develop preliminary discussions which could avoid unnecessary conflict about the proposed project. The game plan was to win regulatory approval by autumn 1990.

RESEARCH

The unhappy experience of Texaco Canada only a short while before convinced LASMO and their consultants that success would depend largely on satisfying the concerns of the fishermen and the environmentalists. The spring 1989 edition of the Decima Quarterly published a survey of Canadian public opinion by one of Canada's foremost research organisations, which reported that the environment was the top concern among Canadians. Respondents believed that government involvement in environmental issues was necessary and over one-third had little confidence in oil companies.

This widely-read report was not a good basis on which to plan the campaign. In order to assess the underlying problems facing LASMO, careful scrutiny was made of published materials, including environmental assessments of the Texaco project, and in-depth interviews were conducted with ten experts representing academia, the Government, the larger commercial fishery, the independent fishery, the media, the oil industry and the environmental lobby. The results of these interviews were most informative and helped to form the basis for strategic planning.

From the research study and the interviews, it was concluded that LASMO's project need not suffer the same fate as Texaco's if LASMO could demonstrate beyond doubt that the project would not harm the environment. It was clear that LASMO must meet and successfully negotiate with the fishing community to prevent their organised opposition to the project which could kill any hope of success.

PLANNING

Before any detailed planning could be undertaken, it was necessary to identify the major sources of powerful opposition. The strategy adopted was to obviate opposition in advance rather than to try to meet it when it erupted. The target audiences were identified as the independent and commercial fisheries, and the federal, provincial and local governments. Not everybody would be against the scheme and one potential powerful ally could be the Offshore Trade Association. The news media might also be helpful if approached at an early stage and fully briefed.

The key messages

Four key messages were developed for the target audiences:

1. Oil from Cohasset and Panuke is extremely light, having the colour and consistency of a cup of weak tea.
2. The proposed production area is not heavily fished, is ice free and the seas are relatively calm.
3. LASMO's project is quite small, costing less than five per cent of the estimated cost for the Hibernia development planned for the North Atlantic off Newfoundland.
4. The production technology to be used for the project has been used successfully all over the world, so no new technological innovations are required.

Media relations

LASMO were advised not to make any general public announcement or to file any applications, which would automatically initiate public hearings, until productive discussions had been concluded with the identified opinion leaders. LASMO were advised to respond to media enquiries by emphasising the four key messages, but not to seek any publicity. In discussions with journalists, LASMO were advised to avoid discussion of any definitive programme or schedule, emphasising that everything would depend on the results of the preliminary discussions and the review process.

The reason for trying to avoid early media interest was the desire to prevent precipitative concern that the scheme would pose a threat to both the fishery and the environment. It was hoped that, in due course, the story would be treated as an energy story and an oil industry achievement.

Implementation

In lieu of public meetings, the most senior LASMO executives met privately with fishery and environmental groups and with government officials, at both political and bureaucratic levels. During these meetings, LASMO executives listened first and then communicated the key messages. LASMO's credibility was enhanced by its early agreement to a comprehensive compensation plan for fishermen, in which any claims would be assessed by an independent group representing both the petroleum and the fishing industries.

An information pack highlighting the key messages was prepared for use as required, but no broadly based circulation was sought.

Media training was provided for LASMO executives and they were advised to seek one-to-one interviews, rather than news conferences.

EVALUATION

In September 1990, the Canada-Nova Scotia Offshore Petroleum Board approved LASMO's application to produce oil at Cohasset and Panuke. This would be Canada's first commercial offshore oil production.

There was no organised opposition to the project during the 18 months of LASMO's operations, thanks to the careful approach and intelligent strategy. The approval date of September 1990 was consistent with LASMO's internal project schedule.

An editorial in the region's leading daily newspaper, the *Chronicle-Herald*, commented:

LASMO took the lessons of Texaco's experience to heart ....
If LASMO had not taken so much pains to address the concerns of fishermen, it would not now be well on its way towards producing oil in Canada's first commercial offshore project.

The first oil came ashore on 5 June 1992, and was welcomed by the community. A report in the *Daily News* of 6 June 1992 (see Figure 3) was typical of the many welcoming stories.

A reception was held to mark the occasion and a commemorative plaque was unveiled. Comment in the press was very supportive and the event was hailed as a wonderful step forward in the economic development of Nova Scotia. Typical newspaper headlines were: 'Offshore oil project fascinating and welcome'; 'Let it flow'; 'After 30 years it's offshore oil'.

CASE DISCUSSION

This programme received the overall award of excellence in the 1991 International Public Relations Association Golden World Awards for Excellence. It was a very good example of how the quiet and gentle approach will often be more successful than a major frontal attack.

There are many lessons to be learnt from this case. Because one

After 30 years, it's offshore oil

'Historic moment' sees output begin from Panuke-Cohasset

By BRIAN FLINN
The Daily News

Canada's first and long-awaited commercial offshore oil project is now in production, LASMO Nova Scotia Ltd. announced at a news conference yesterday in Halifax.

After two years of work and a $300 million investment by LASMO and its 50/50 partner Nova Scotia Resources Ltd. (NSRL), the Panuke-Cohasset oil project started pumping oil at 8 a.m. yesterday at a rate of 14,000 barrels a day.

"This is the first commercial production of oil from Canada's offshore and represents an historic moment for our country," said LASMO's executive vice president and general manager Norm Miller.

"After more than 30 years of oil industry investment in offshore exploration, income from production has finally been achieved. Production from the Cohasset project is now a reality."

Panuke-Cohasset will directly provide 400 full-time jobs, 75 per cent of them in Nova Scotia and 90 per cent in Canada, he said.

$300 million before production and an estimated $90 million in the first year — would make the project feasible even if world oil prices fall to $20 US a barrel. The benchmark North Sea Brent oil is now at about $21.25 US a barrel.

"I'd would be very happy (if oil stayed at) current levels, I'd be happier if they rise," said Miller. "The project is comfortable anywhere around $20 a barrel.

Tanker transfer

The oil, a light, sweet crude with the color and consistency of whisky or tea, is now being pumped into a holding tanker, the Nordic Apollo, and will be transferred to a shuttle tanker in July. The oil will then be transported to a refinery in Mobile, Ala.

Miller said the oil will be sold to the highest bidder, and he doesn't expect that will allow any to be landed in Atlantic Canada. Refineries here are configured for heavier Venezuelan crude and would have to go through costly modifications to process the lighter oil.

Figure 3 Example of a newspaper report welcoming the success of the scheme

project has failed dismally, it does not necessarily follow that another rather similar scheme is going to be equally unsuccessful. The warning of the previous failure should be an additional spur to analyse very carefully the reasons for the other debacle. This is exactly what Ian Thompson did in his preliminary feasibility study. He identified the crucial factor which was that the opposition would be too strong unless the fishermen's acquiescence could be secured before the formal approval procedures began.

It is relevant to quote from the 'Communications Strategy Overview' prepared by Ian Thompson in September 1989. It made six important recommendations:

1. In our view, it is essential to begin discussions immediately with fishing interests and specifically on the subject of a compensation plan.
2. We wish to stress that there is some urgency to initiating these discussions. Fishing interests will not regard negotiations as being sincere if they are held simultaneously with a development application being moved through the bureaucracy.
3. We must enter the negotiations without fixed and final views. We must be willing to give and take. These fishing groups have legitimate concerns and they have much to contribute.
4. Our approach in these initial meetings should be to provide only a general overview of our proposal with some sense of the design/operational options we may have before us.
5. We believe these discussions should be handled at the highest practical level on our side, with the support of a consultant from outside the petroleum industry with a favourable reputation among fishing interests.
6. We believe key members of the management team should participate in a media training programme.

These initial proposals were accepted by LASMO and were the basis of the whole public relations programme which achieved success. Figure 4 is a copy of the news release sent out by LASMO in triumph. This a very good example of a suitable release, giving the whole story together with relevant facts and statistics.

FIRST OFFSHORE OIL

News release

LASMO Nova Scotia Limited
Suite 1400 Founders Square
1701 Hollis Street, Halifax
Nova Scotia B3J 3M8, Canada
Telephone 902 · 422 4500
Facsimile 902 · 425 2766

For Immediate Release
June 5, 1992

LASMO ANNOUNCES FIRST COMMERCIAL OIL
PRODUCTION FROM OFFSHORE CANADA

LASMO Nova Scotia, a subsidiary of LASMO plc, announced today that it has achieved first commercial oil production offshore Canada from its Cohasset development project, located some 250 kilometres southeast of Halifax, Nova Scotia.

The Cohasset success represents a major step in a 30 year quest by national and international companies to establish commercial oil production from Canada's vast offshore areas. LASMO's achievement is the first of its kind.

LASMO Nova Scotia is operator for the Cohasset project, and has a 50 per cent interest as does its partner Nova Scotia Resources Limited (NSRL), a Provincial Crown Corporation based in Halifax.

The Cohasset development comprises two offshore fields, Cohasset and Panuke, which have estimated recoverable oil reserves of approximately 50 million barrels. The oil is light and of high quality which attracts a premium price in the world market.

Initial production has commenced from the Panuke field only and oil is being processed on the jack-up platform Rowan Gorilla III (RGIII), a combined drilling and production facility. It is then loaded into an offshore storage tanker, the Nordic Apollo, before being shipped to North American refineries by the shuttle tanker, Nordic Challenger.

In 1993 the RGIII will commence development drilling in the Cohasset field, as a result of which total production is expected to rise to approximately 40,000 barrels per day. At a later stage a third field, Balmoral, a small satellite located some three kilometres northeast of the existing facilities, will be tied into Cohasset by subsea pipeline.

Figure 4 News release announcing that oil was flowing

Case 2.2 Teamwork Arkansas

BACKGROUND

The genesis of the 'Teamwork Arkansas' programme was the premise that large businesses operating in the state of Arkansas should play a leading role in the economic development of the state.

The state's largest electric utility company, Arkansas Power & Light (AP&L) recognised that a major commitment to industrial development would be a wise investment in the future of Arkansas and the economic vitality of its service area. AP&L also recognised that it was one of the few corporations in the state with the scope and the resources to make a lasting impact on improvements in the state's economy and in establishing new jobs for Arkansas.

The results of research indicated that AP&L customers wanted to see their electric utility company become involved in the economic development of the state. Based on the findings of this research, the objective of 'Teamwork Arkansas' was to build a stronger economic base in Arkansas which would help to provide more jobs for the citizens of the state and to focus positive attention on AP&L for leading this effort.

PLANNING

AP&L chairman Jerry Maulden announced 'Teamwork Arkansas' at a news conference in April 1987 at the State Capitol. Governor Clinton (now President Clinton) and top business and community leaders were present. Maulden said that the five-year $10–15 million programme would be one of the most comprehensive economic development efforts by the private sector in the nation.

From the beginning of 1989 to the first half of 1991, the action and growth of 'Teamwork Arkansas' was evidenced by the number of job expansion schemes announced during the period – an average of nearly three per week. Planning and strategy focused on three main areas:

1. a broad based effort of national and international prospecting;
2. state-wide community development; and
3. state-wide and national advertising and public relations initiatives to promote Arkansas.

The total programme budget for 1990 was approximately $3 million, including professional staffing, industrial recruiting trips, community development, trade show participation and all operating expenses. Production and media for paid advertising totalled approximately $500,000.

Audiences of the 'Teamwork' effort were divided into two main categories: audiences within Arkansas and those outside the state. In-state audiences included customers of AP&L, business and political leaders of local communities, managers of existing industries and leaders in public education and the academic community.

IMPLEMENTATION

In-state audiences saw and heard a series of print and broadcast advertisements designed to generate new enthusiasm for economic growth in the state. In addition, advertisements were placed encouraging Arkansas business to 'buy Arkansas' products and services where feasible.

The city of Glenwood became the first Arkansas community to complete AP&L's 'Teamwork' community development training programme called 'Leadership Arkansas'. This was celebrated by a special governor's reception at the Governor's Mansion. 'Leadership Arkansas' training was also conducted in Jacksonville, Arkadelphia, Marshall and Crosset, and was planned to continue in other Arkansas communities during the next two years.

Teamwork Arkansas Magazine was created as the primary information source and focal point of the programme. This is a quarterly, full colour publication that provides information on new jobs and development progress in Arkansas. Articles in the magazine tell success stories of entrepreneurs, corporations, the Arkansas Industrial Development Commission and other forces contributing to economic growth in the state. During the first year, more than 12,000 of the state's leaders in business, government and education, as well as industrial prospects across the nation and overseas, received quarterly issues of the magazine.

EVALUATION

Since 'Teamwork Arkansas' began, 135 companies announced that they would build a new plant in AP&L's service area and 277 companies announced expansions that, when completed, would result in more than 38,000 new jobs – ie more than 12 new jobs a day. 'Teamwork Arkansas' results were recognised and the programme gained even greater visibility in October 1990 when it received the J William Fulbright Award for International Trade from the Mid-South Trade Association. A solid public relations programme ensured that this prestigious honour was featured prominently in the news media.

To sum up, 'Teamwork Arkansas' was bringing new jobs and new enterprises to the state through advertising, the new magazine and the sound public relations programme.

CASE DISCUSSION

This case is an example of a leading organisation in a country or state taking a lead to mobilise the support of other interested bodies to combat a common challenge to their joint prosperity. This report makes a passing reference to the support that the programme received from the state governor who has since become President of the United States. Does this mean that public relations will receive increased respect from the White House?

The report shows how a professionally planned and executed programme can gain wide public support and yield excellent results. The campaign received very good support from the media and this was probably due to the fact that the programme was initiated and progressed by one of the state's largest organisations. The following quotation from an editorial in a leading Arkansas newspaper illustrates this active support:

> It is obvious from state government budget problems that an economic shot in the arm is needed. More power to *Teamwork Arkansas* for trying to administer the development vaccine.

This term 'development vaccine' is a fine example of inspired imagery which could be used elsewhere to advantage in connection with similar programmes.

Another aspect of this type of programme is the value of a good logo. The logo used by 'Teamwork Arkansas' is shown in Figure 5. This logo could be criticised as being too fussy and complicated. A fair comment, but this logo is distinctive, puts over its message clearly and even advertises AP&L which put up millions of dollars to finance the scheme.

Schemes like this, advocating development schemes of one kind or another, are basically economic ones, but despite the fact that advertising usually features prominently in the programme, it is public relations analysis and leadership that ensures success. In this case, an Arkansas public relations agency, Cranford Johnson Robinson Woods, was engaged by Arkansas Power & Light to plan and administer the programme.

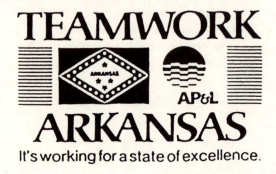

Figure 5 The TEAMWORK ARKANSAS logo

3

Protecting the Environment

Case 3.1 Protecting the global environment

BACKGROUND

This case study describes the work of the Industry Cooperative for Ozone Layer Protection (ICOLP) which was formed in 1989 to speed up the elimination of ozone-depleting technologies and thus help to preserve the earth's atmospheric layer. It works by encouraging and coordinating the open, world-wide exchange of information on technologies to replace *chlorofluorocarbons* (CFCs) and other ozone-depleting substances.

ICOLP is a unique global partnership of industry and governments formed to identify alternative technologies and to promote their transfer to countries and companies which need them. ICOLP is an innovative and practical contribution to solving a major environmental problem, as well as a working model of cooperative action applicable to other environmental problems. ICOLP is administered by the E Bruce Harrison Company Inc of Washington DC.

RESEARCH

Seventy-four nations and international organisations signed the 1987 Montreal Protocol on substances that deplete the ozone layer. This treaty restricts the production and use of ozone-depleting chemicals and mandates the complete elimination of the most potent ones by the year 2000 or shortly thereafter. It is the result of scientific research implicating CFCs in the thinning of stratospheric ozone, and the realisation by industry and governments world-wide that severe health and environmental problems might follow.

The problem was that until recently, CFCs – inert, non-inflammable, non-toxic and inexpensive — seemed to be the perfect chemicals. They have been used extensively in many critical applications, from solvents and blowing agents to air conditioning and refrigerant coolants. They have made whole technologies and industries possible. The daunting challenge now facing industry is to find a substitute to replace this seemingly irreplaceable class of chemicals.

The response from several forward thinking industrial users of CFCs was to make commitments to eliminate their use as soon as possible and begin an intensive search for alternatives. Research and consultation by individual companies revealed that alternative technologies existed for specific applications but that much refinement was necessary. It also became clear that the search for these alternatives would be time-consuming and technically difficult, even for large companies with vast resources. The problem would be even more acute for smaller companies and those without access to technical information, which would make it nearly impossible to make the transition. The problem would be even more difficult in less developed countries where up-to-date technical libraries are rare.

PLANNING

In an effort to solve these problems in the relatively short time available, a group of large US electronic and aerospace companies joined together with the US Environmental Protection Agency. The group's objectives were to form an organisation and to create the means to help accelerate their own phase-out of CFCs and to promote the open, world-wide exchange of information on technologies to replace CFCs and other ozone-depleting substances, particularly their use as solvents in the electronic and aerospace industries.

It was clearly necessary to gather information on usable technologies and to set up a mechanism to provide easy access to the data. The information needed to be instantly and globally available through credible institutions to be of any use. Access costs had to be kept down so that small companies and those in less developed countries could easily tap into the information. The ICOLP organisers saw that these objectives could be achieved through an international organisation drawing on both private and public resources. The membership of major multinational corporations, coupled with participation by government agencies, would ease world-wide communication about alternative technologies and hasten their adoption. Participation by these groups would also ensure the technical expertise necessary to allow the development of easily used and widely accessible data sources. The E Bruce Harrison Company was selected to carry out the programme because of its extensive experience in managing environmental issues.

The cost of achieving these objectives would be covered by the actual membership dues for membership, set at $25,000 per company, and in-kind contributions from participating organisations.

IMPLEMENTATION

Formally constituted as ICOLP, the group, in coordination with the E Bruce Harrison Company, began an aggressive membership campaign in which officers of member companies contacted their peers in other companies and encouraged them to join. Key selling points were that members could demonstrate publicly their commitment to protecting the environment while showing that voluntary industry and government partnership can work to solve environmental problems.

In less than two years, ICOLP's membership expanded to include AT&T, Boeing, British Aerospace, Compaq Computer, Digital Equipment, Ford, General Electric, Hitachi, Honeywell, IBM, Matsushita, Motorola, Northern Telecom, Sundstrand, Texas Instruments and Toshiba. ICOLP also signed formal Memoranda of Understanding (MOU) with the US Environmental Protection Agency, the United States Air Force, the USSR State Institute of Applied Chemistry, the Swedish National Environmental Protection Agency, the Japan Electrical Manufacturers Association, the Electronic Industries Association and the City of Irvine, California. A MOU was also being negotiated with the government of Mexico.

Out of all the available means of disseminating information — newsletters, periodic conferences, exhibitions, etc — it was clear that an electronic database was best suited to meeting the need for instant, world-wide access. Thus was born OZONET, a global database that functions as a clearing house for alternative technologies. Figure 6 describes the OZONET fact sheet.

OZONET can be accessed from more than 90 per cent of the world's business telephones, and all the technical information entered into the database is available free. ICOLP has fully funded the database, users pay only on-line charges to cover the system's

OZONET
FACT SHEET

- **OZONET, created by the Industry Cooperative for Ozone Layer Protection, is an on-line, international (computerized) database designed to provide users of CFC compounds with information on substitute processes, materials and technologies.**

- **The database resides in the General Electric Information Services network and is accessible from more than 750 cities in 35 countries worldwide. It can be accessed from more than 90 percent of the world's business telephones.**

- **Several types of information are available through OZONET:**
    - **Technical**—information on alternative processes, materials, technologies.
    - **Chemical properties**—chemical, physical, toxicological and additional properties.
    - **Supplier information**—products available to the industry.
    - **Events**—upcoming conferences and technology transfer seminars.
    - **Legislation**—treaties, agreements and other pertinent legislation.
    - **Contacts**—key people in government, industry and ICOLP member companies, with addresses, telephone numbers and additional information.

- **OZONET employs an icon screen for ease of use. Users can also pose questions or comments, and receive responses, from other users or from ICOLP members.**

- **OZONET may be linked in the future to other related databases, such as those managed by the United Nations Environment Program in Paris and Nairobi.**

Figure 6 OZONET fact sheet

direct operating costs. The technologies are non-proprietary and can be used at no cost. (A separate directory in OZONET provides information on proprietary technologies, and contacts for obtaining the rights to use them.)

Additionally, ICOLP and the US National Research Council (NRC) have entered a unique arrangement to identify solutions to the problems that remain in finding alternatives to ozone-depleting substances. The NRC has conducted a series of discussions and a workshop to identify the most promising areas for further research and development. The NRC's report was due to be released to the public as soon as it was completed.

EVALUATION

ICOLP met or exceeded all its initial goals. It has become a fully functioning global enterprise with members and affiliates around the world. ICOLP established formal relationships with powerful diverse organisations in the public and private sector listed earlier in this report. OZONET was taken from a concept to an electronic database operating worldwide in approximately nine months, and is now providing information to companies and countries searching for new technologies. ICOLP and the US Environmental Protection Agency embarked on a series of manuals describing alternative technologies.

ICOLP member companies have made public commitments to eliminate the use of ozone-depleting substances as quickly as possible and are encouraging others to make similar commitments. Northern Telecom plans to phase out all use of CFCs during 1991, Motorola by the end of 1992, IBM in 1993, AT&T and Texas Instruments in 1994, and Matsushita and Toshiba by 1995. Other members have set similar goals.

The Digital Equipment Corporation has made an alternative technology available to the public through ICOLP, the *Digital Augusta Aqueous Microdroplet Cleaning Process*. This process cleans electronic boards and modules without the use of halogenated solvents, and by July 1991, ICOLP had responded to 600 requests for information about it. Other ICOLP members were planning to share similar information.

Northern Telecom, working with ICOLP, signed an agreement with the government of Mexico to help eliminate the use of ozone-depleting substances by Mexican industry. Northern Telecom planned to draw upon its own resources as well as expertise from other ICOLP members and affiliates to conduct symposia and workshops on available alternatives. Company experts are acting as consultants to individual Mexican enterprises in their search for new production methods. Plans were also being considered for expanding this programme into other countries.

The National Research Council prepared a report, requested and funded by ICOLP, on the most promising areas for research and development on innovative alternatives to CFCs and other ozone-depleting substances.

To sum up, the creation of ICOLP triggered an explosion of new developments and information about CFC alternatives and demonstrated that partnerships between government and industry could be effective in solving environmental problems. Besides launching a powerful attack on this specific environmental hazard, this experience has set a precedent that can be readily followed to accelerate the resolution of other environmental issues.

TAILPIECE

Bruce Harrison, chairman of E Bruce Harrison Company of Washington DC, was in charge of the work for ICOLP and has made a special study of environmental issues and how they impinge on public relations which goes back to 1960 when he began working with the chemical industry on environmental communication. He has contributed the following thoughts on the current position.

- Business and industry executives rightly see the environment as one of their biggest and most problematic issues. Company managers world-wide are looking for ways not only to respond to tough green-versus-growth issues but to take charge and step ahead of the pack by going beyond environmental compliance and achieving competitive advantage.
- Environmentalism forces public relations to plough new ground. The 30-year march of the environmental movement has constantly driven the practice of public relations to evolve new strategies and to refine tactics. 'Green' public relations has become a specialty which requires operational consideration by all companies, industries, businesses, professions and governments.
- The roots of this endemic institutional preoccupation with the environment lie in the public's interest in it. Workers, consumers, young people and other groups rate the environment among their gravest concerns. In the United States it has

become a cliché that three-quarters of Americans consider themselves 'environmentalists'. Most have decided they do not trust business to advance their interests in this regard.

- The pivotal media role in this process cannot be ignored. Vivid coverage of environmental disasters and tragedies has created a gallery of memorable images: Love Canal, Santa Barbara, Bhopal, Chernobyl, Prince William Sound, Kuwait. Moreover, the media are seen by some as having become actors in these dramas, not merely reporters of them. Wall Street Journal reporter Amal Kumar Naj has written: '. . . in a remarkable transition, the baton of environmentalism has passed from fence-climbing radicals and fringe groups into the hands of a powerful and credible constituency, the media . . . A number of journalists feel, and rightly so, that if they don't rigorously influence public opinion and force the issue on the business community, nothing will be achieved.'

Thus the context in which environmental issues are discussed is infused with a presumption of peril that makes straightforward communication about otherwise unrelated matters extraordinarily difficult.

Lacking sound advice in the face of these disadvantages, it is easy to falter in a crisis. Clear lessons emerged from the Exxon Valdez incident in March 1989: the CEO makes or breaks the public relations outcome. Like a football goalie, you are only as good as your last 'save'. You can do the right things technically and still lose the public relations game. Above all, the human drama is far more important than science, logic or even the facts.

How can public relations professionals help? Rutgers University Professor Peter Sandman says that the best the risk communicator can do is to help management understand why certain publics are worried about certain products or practices. It is a job well suited to the public relations practitioner, whose charge is not merely to convey information to different publics but to build public relationships. This requires discourse and interaction, keeping our fingers on the public pulse and interpreting that pulse to managers.

Pollution is now an evil. While everybody contributes, business and industry are seen as the devil's special henchmen. Business, says the public 'does it to us, we are the victims'. In contrast, effective business executives will see green and growth as a rapidly widening interface where the central task is harmonising the most important social and business trend of the 1990s and the necessity of management to create customers, to compete and to succeed.

CASE DISCUSSION

The environment and related considerations provide a fertile ground for public relations practitioners. This exists on many different levels. The case study of ICOLP describes the multinational and governmental level, but the essential need to monitor 'green' issues exists at every level of business and industry. If management receives accurate and anticipatory interpretations of public fears and desires, as well as good counsel on ways to change policies or procedures, public relations practitioners will be as much in demand to deal with environmental issues as with media relations.

Some manufacturers have claimed 'green' virtues for products and services which are quite unaffected by such considerations. This tendency to 'exaggeration' is as much counter-productive as inflated advertising claims and is harmful to reputation and credibility.

Case 3.2 Managing forests and vast nature reserves

This is an account of the successful total communications programme carried out by the Swedish Domän Group from 1988 to 1991.

The Group had long played a key role in the management of Swedish forests and providing public facilities for outdoor life. About 20 per cent of the total area of Sweden, including considerable parts of the country's nature reserves, were administered by Domän with its 5500 employees and a turnover of £350 million.

In the early 1980s, the reputation of Domän was fairly negative, partly due to widespread criticism of Swedish forestry methods. This was reflected by poor morale within the organisation. A new director general and CEO, Mr Bo Hedstrom, was appointed, and with the help of his new executive team he decided to make a positive effort to restore Domän's reputation by systematic communication with key target groups and with the general public. A position of vice-president, public relations was created in 1986 with a seat in the Domän executive group.

In that new executive group, a series of decisions with long-range consequences for Domän was taken, including a reorganisation with reduced staff at headquarters and with more responsibility being left to the forestry districts. Of great significance to the public relations function were the decisions to ban the use of herbicides in 1986, to change towards a more ecologically-oriented forestry, including the training of 1000 foresters in a special programme called 'Our forests are threatened', and to make a strong commitment to environmental and opinion-building activities. Public relations planning was integrated into the total budget and planning process of Domän, and a dialogue on public relations issues started with all resource unit members of the Group.

THE STARTING POINT

Opinion polls in 1988 showed that Swedish forestry management was quite unpopular and misunderstood. Only 20 per cent of

Swedes knew that the annual increase in Swedish forests was greater than the volume felled. Nearly half the population believed that the forests were sprayed with pesticides every year, although spraying with herbicides had been prohibited since 1986.

Public opinion expected and demanded Domän, as state owned, to be more environment conscious than the forestry industries. The group was expected not only to produce and deliver the best possible raw material to the pulp and sawmill industries, but also to care about the multitude of wildlife, to safeguard wilderness areas, to provide good fishing and hunting possibilities, and at the same time to be more conscious of the environment than all its competitors – a very delicate balancing act.

A COMMUNICATIONS PLATFORM

A 'communications platform' was agreed upon by the Domän executive group, including the following key elements:

1. The management philosophy shall permeate all information work.
2. Devotion and understanding by all employees of the aims and direction of the Group is one of the most important conditions for success.
3. The managers shall seize every opportunity for encouragement, but, with their staffs, find out the reasons for any failure to reach the Group's objectives and draw the correct conclusions.
4. Internal discussion and debate is an important prerequisite to making the right decisions and for the staff to feel at ease and to enjoy job satisfaction.
5. We should benefit from the advantages of size but act towards individuals and organisations in such a way that they do not feel they are running against a colossus. Whenever necessary, we shall admit to shortcomings in our work in an open manner.

PLANNING

It was agreed that the public relations policy to be adopted could be summed up as: 'The Domän group combines demands for profitability with strict environmental control and an active contribution to outdoor life – the so-called 'multiple use concept'. Initial concentration would be on communicating with both employees and the general public. This policy was enshrined in a three-year plan, 1988–1990, 'The communication platform and the verbal identity'.

In order to help managers at all levels in their communication work a document was produced: 'The public relations tools – aids to information and public relations work within the Domän Group'. This document was essentially a do-it-yourself public relations handbook for beginners, with step-by-step advice on everything from oral communication with forestry workers to tips on media relations. A series of seminars for 400 line managers helped to implement positive public relations thinking throughout the organisation.

New life was breathed into the company's house journal *Domänposten* and the contents changed from light reading and gossip to concentration on results, working methods and prospects.

Pilot projects for communication with a few local committees were tested, with a view to a wider implementation later. Such efforts were, of course, dependent on the degree to which regional and local managers were prepared to accept public relations as a vital part of their responsibilities and as a strategic management instrument, in competition with other time-consuming managerial tasks.

These managers had a good story to tell their public. In tune with changing public opinion, Swedish forestry had committed itself to combating acid rain and air pollution problems. One thousand foresters had been trained by university teams to adopt a more ecology-conscious programme. Domän maintained 1500 fishing waters and 40 non-commercial areas open to the public.

INFORMATION POLICY

The new communication handbook emphasised that internal information should have top priority. All employees directly affected by events or changes, within or outside Domän, should be informed about these and their positive or negative consequences. Active contacts with authorities, politicians, institutions, schools and other target groups should be established and developed with a view to exerting influence on working conditions.

All recreation areas and public areas were used as information centres to spread information about Domän and its positive policy of promptness, sincerity and coordination. Regular contact with the public is secured through its annual wall calendar *Nature och Fritid* (nature and leisure). This calendar includes selected facts about Domän and encourages readers to contact Domän Turist about the choice of leisure time activities offered by Domän. Above all, however, the calendar offers 12 exquisite photographs of Swedish nature during the four seasons of the year. The circulation of the calendar is 2.2 million to a total Swedish population of 8.5 million. A Gallup poll in 1990 showed that as many as 700,000 calendars were hanging on the walls of offices and homes.

The best-selling publications of Domän, however, are its leisure time folders. About 40 non-commercial recreation areas are presented in separate A6 size folders with maps, basic facts about sites of special interest and brief information about Domän. Several million copies of these folders are distributed each year, mainly through the state and municipal tourist offices.

Fishing in the Domän waters is available for anyone who pays a small licence fee. To encourage and inform fishing enthusiasts, the quarterly *Domänfiske* (Domän Fishing) is produced by the group, and about 70,000 Swedes renew their fishing licences annually and get information on fish, fishing and Domän through this magazine.

Information for schools and students is prepared by the Domän public relations department dealing with such subjects as *Our Forest; The Seedling; The Tree.*

EVALUATION

At the end of the three-year programme, 1988–1990, some basic results of the work could be measured and evaluated.

1. Compared with the leading forest industries, Domän had left its bottom ranking and had achieved the top position with regard to both knowledge and attitude.
2. Out of 8.5 million inhabitants in Sweden, probably 50 per cent were reached by the magazine Nature and Leisure, and 700,000 calendars are displayed on walls.
3. Domän registered over 25 million day-visits per year to its recreation areas.
4. Through the Domän catalogue, 575,000 nights were booked in the Domän holiday cottages.
5. 70,000 fishing enthusiasts registered and purchased fishing licences for the Domän lakes and waters.
6. The house journal received very favourable marks in externally conducted reader polls despite, or thanks to, the new editorial policy of including more business news. The journal won first prize for its front cover in a competition among all Swedish house journals.

CASE DISCUSSION

On 1 July 1992, the whole picture changed due to a reorganisation which turned Domän into a limited company, prior to later flotation on the Stock Exchange. This change of company structure meant that the public relations of the group would, in many respects, have to be restarted. The success achieved during 1988–90, on an annual budget of £2 million, with a staff of six will, however, form an excellent model for the partly new company to follow.

This case study received a golden award in the 1990 IPRA Golden World Awards for Excellence. Acknowledgement is due to Lars-Olle Larsson who, as senior vice-president, public relations for Domän during the period discussed, was in charge of the planning and implementation. He is now senior vice-president, public relations of Sweden Post.

This account of the radical changes at Domän illustrates the many different ways in which public relations can play an important part in the restructuring and repositioning of a large corporation. The management of change is often an important part of public relations activities and the many differences of emphasis at Domän, consequent on the appointment of a new director general, certainly provided many challenges in this regard.

The Domän story is included in this chapter dealing with the environment since the activities of Domän are directly related to the way a country deals with its ecological and environmental resources, problems and opportunities. It could equally well have been included in the chapter on corporate relations, since it illustrates the positive part played by the public relations policy in the restructuring of the organisation. Chapter 4, dealing with employee relations and communication, could also have been a suitable home for this case study as reading the report emphasises the attention which was devoted to improving employee morale and motivation.

The explanation is simple. Public relations is not confined to any one part of business or commercial life. At Domän, the vice-president's public relations played an active role on the executive management team, helping to reposition the future strategy of the organisation, but he was also responsible for many practical tasks including media relations, the revamped publications and the publicity of the company.

Case 3.3 We do Kare

BACKGROUND

In 1987, Bayer Australia acquired a chemical plant at Wyong operating as Kemcon Pty Ltd. Bayer invested A$12.5 million in upgrading the plant, with A$2.5 million of this investment being allocated to environmental protection and safety systems.

Despite the company's efforts to make this plant one of the most sophisticated and environmentally safe plants of its kind in Australia, by 1989 the plant was receiving frequent unfavourable local media coverage.

The source of these attacks was a small local action group known as CCAC (Central Coast Against Chemicals) which had enjoyed a previous success in stopping a large multinational chemical company (Ashlands) from establishing a plant in the Wyong area. CCAC feared that emissions from the Kemcon plant would disturb the sensitive flora and fauna of the adjoining wetlands which feed the Tuggerah Lakes system. Other concerns expressed centred on the risk of fire or explosions involving flammable materials and chemicals.

The CCAC took steps in 1989 to present the case against Bayer to the Land and Environment Court. Success of this action would have meant the closure of the plant and the forced relocation of Bayer formulation facilities. This was the beginning of what was to be a series of confrontations, actions and resolutions between Bayer, the CCAC and the Wyong Shire Council from 1989 to 1993.

Professional Public Relations Pty Ltd (PPR) was engaged by Bayer in November 1989 to research the issues existing at Kemcon and to make recommendations for managing these issues. In January 1990, PPR was retained by Bayer to implement the recommended three-year plan.

The plan recommended and implemented bears the mark of a classic textbook public relations exercise. From day one, when the preliminary research revealed vital information not known to the client, the stage was set for the implementation of a programme designed not only to change the company culture, but in so doing to address the short- and long-term needs of the company.

RESEARCH

The research programme was conducted under six categories.

1. Information was gathered and analysed on the local action group CCAC together with personal profiles of its office holders: president, secretary and publicity officer. Past successes of the group and the strategies employed were thoroughly researched and analysed.
2. An employee climate study was conducted within the Kemcon operation which provided direction for both in-house and external communication activities. This study unearthed some unexpected aspects of internal relations.
3. All available research on the Wyong community was gathered and assessed with particular attention paid to the fact that a previous community action group's opposition to a chemical company had been successful.
4. Previous actions of the Wyong Council with regard to rezoning were researched, documented and assessed.
5. Media research over 1989, particularly into the previous CCAC action against Ashlands, gave some indication of the strategies employed and the personalities involved.
6. Continuing research was conducted into employee attitudes, through questionnaires, analysis of media clippings and feedback through the staff newsletter.

PLANNING

The results of the comprehensive research study indicated the communication strategies which PPR should adopt and the appropriate goals and objectives.

Goals and objectives

1. **Short term**
   i) To attempt to head off impending action in the Land and Environment Court.
   ii) To take steps to improve staff morale and productivity.
   iii) To make positive efforts to replace negative media coverage with news of Kemcon/Bayer's efforts to preserve the environment.
2. **Long term**
   i) To combat the activities of the local action group.

ii) To position the Kemcon plant as an integral, productive, environmentally safe and welcome part of the Wyong community.

Target publics

In order to keep the whole programme within manageable limits, it was necessary to establish the target publics. This was done under eight headings.

1. Kemcon employees, their families, friends and neighbours.
2. 'Neighbours' – other companies operating alongside Kemcon in the Wyong Industrial Estate.
3. The Wyong Shire councillors and local council employees.
4. Local services – fire brigade, police, ambulance service, etc.
5. Representatives of the local and state government.
6. Schools within the Shire.
7. The Wyong general community.
8. Employees of Kemcon's parent company, Bayer Australia, their families, friends and neighbours.

Communication strategies

The action plan adopted was directed to the achievement of both short- and long-term objectives. The most urgent needs would be addressed first.

Recognising that the staff of Kemcon, their families and friends could be harnessed as a vital resource for the proposed community education programme, PPR adopted a strategy to make use of the Kemcon staff of more than 120 people as the primary vehicle to promote the facts about Kemcon to the target publics.

A six-month internal communication programme was planned, which would be implemented and then adapted and taken to 'neighbours', councillors and action groups.

IMPLEMENTATION

Timetable

The following timetable was adopted:

● **January to June (year one)**
  Internal communication programme.
● **July to December (year one)**

Wyong Community communication programme — action groups, councillors and 'neighbours'.
- **January (year two and continuing)**
  Wider community communication programme.

Internal communication — January to June (year one)

This internal communication strategy provided the solid base on which PPR built the 'community' and 'general public' communication programmes which followed.

Advisory committee

An employee advisory committee was set up to launch the internal communication programme. The committee was made up of staff (non-management) from each department of Kemcon, one representative of Kemcon management and one from Bayer management. The committee was chaired by PPR, minutes were recorded and distributed.

The immediate task of the committee was to:

- provide information on staff attitudes to the issues;
- assess staff attitudes to the company;
- create a theme for the programme;
- contribute to the inaugural monthly newsletter;
- deliver ideas for competitions;
- assist in organising the launch of the programme.

Researching staff attitudes

During the information gathering phase, it became apparent that internal relationships, particularly between the plant general manager and all levels of staff, were in urgent need of attention.

This finding was unexpected as no part of the client brief indicated a potential staff relations problem of this kind. The consultancy recommended the selection of an industrial psychologist to assess the situation.

This work during the early months of the programme resulted in a senior management change with significant ramifications. It improved staff relations, credibility and acceptance of management's concern and favourable receipt of the internal communication programme.

Figure 7 Logo for the Kemcon internal communications
programme

Internal communication – January to June (year one)

Creating a theme
The advisory committee selected the theme for the programme.
PPR designed the logo (see Figure 7) and video and wrote the jingle
around the theme.

Because the programme was to be employee driven, it was
important that the theme should come from the employee group.
'We do Kare' was one of 22 themes nominated by the employees. It
was voted on by the committee and chosen as the winner.

Internal monthly newsletter
PPR created and edited the *KC News* staff newsletter. Each month,
all employees were given the opportunity to contribute. Family
contribution was encouraged with a special 'Kids Corner' section
and birthday wishes for staff members' families.

The newsletter progressed during the six-month period from a
very staff-based format (80 per cent staff news and 20 per cent
company news) to one which included responsible items on safety,
the environment and product stories (50 per cent staff news and 50
per cent company news).

Launch of the programme
The Kemcon 'We do Kare' programme was launched to all Kemcon
staff at a local club venue.

Theme give-aways, including T-shirts, stickers, newsletters and
coasters, were distributed that evening. Refreshments were
provided.

The managing director of Bayer informed employees on the

current situation with action groups, the local council, legal issues, etc.

PPR explained the internal communication programme and how it fitted in with the broader public relations strategy. The evening, which was compèred by a local radio personality, had three objectives: to provide information, to motivate and to encourage participation.

Video

A video was produced based around the theme and featuring the specially written jingle. Fifty per cent of the staff participated and 70 per cent appeared in the video.

The video was particularly well received at the launch function. Proof of its popularity was the immediate request from staff to purchase copies – 40 were sold to staff – and 20 were given away in competitions.

The video was later adapted and used for the community awareness programme.

The video continues to be used as part of Kemcon's new employee induction programme.

Summary of the results of the internal programme

Early research had indicated that Kemcon employees were often having to defend themselves for working at Kemcon and many would deny working at Kemcon when tackled in social situations.

The 'We do Kare' theme chosen by the employees had broad appeal to the majority of employees and helped to revive their pride in Kemcon. The theme conveyed the message that Kemcon was a good place in which to work and that the company had many worthwhile benefits for the community.

Lines of communication were opened within the company which had never been experienced before. As a result:

- the newsletter receives more contributions than it can print;
- a staff social club was formed and regular staff and family functions are organised by this group;
- a 'worker liaison committee' was formed which continues to meet regularly with representatives from both management and 'the floor';
- staff voluntarily and actively participate in the Community Awareness programme which followed.

Wyong Community and Council – July to December (year one)

During this period the strategy addressed the need to open lines of communication between Kemcon and all those likely to be involved in the Kemcon issue. These target groups included community action groups, councillors and 'neighbours'.

Land and Environmental Court Action
Meetings between Bayer and CCAC resulted in the withdrawal of court action by the CCAC. An agreement was reached which provided that a monitoring committee be established and that Bayer should lodge an environmental impact statement and a rezoning application with Wyong Council.

Community-based monitoring committee
This committee meets bimonthly, with representatives from CCAC, Wyong Council, local emergency services, Bayer and Kemcon management.

A procedure was established by this committee which provided that in the event of a chemical spill or accident at the plant, members of the committee should be informed first and given a full explanation of the occurrence and how it was handled.

This procedure was tested within six weeks of the committee's establishment and resulted in one of the first positive media reports, with endorsement from the CCAC about the effectiveness of the committee and Kemcon's responsible attitude and open dialogue approach.

Wyong Community and Council – July to December (year one)

An 'open day' Christmas function was held in December (year one) to which all neighbours (companies in the industrial estate), Wyong councillors and action groups were invited to a social function and plant tours.

A dialogue and mutual trust has developed between Kemcon and its 'neighbours' which was evidenced when several 'neighbours' advised Kemcon that they had been approached by the local action group, CCAC, requesting an opportunity to speak to their staff. Two of these 'neighbours' actually offered to record the proceedings for Kemcon.

Newsletter
The distribution of the Kemcon employee newsletter *KC News* was broadened to inform 'neighbours' and other target publics from December (year one) onwards.

The wider community — January (year two and continuing)

Methods/active involvement

The lodging of the environmental impact statement (EIS), development application and rezoning application to the council attracted the attention of Greenpeace (as was predicted) which in turn revitalised the local action groups.

An aggressive campaign against Kemcon was launched and media coverage again reached its 1989 pitch. The advantage this time, however, was that Kemcon had the support of its staff and the 'neighbours' and had established open dialogue with local action groups.

The strategy was to provide the wider community, the 'silent majority' of Wyong Shire residents, with access to information about Kemcon without appearing to be fighting or confronting the action group CCAC.

Information centres

Information centres were set up over a three-month period in various shopping centres in the Wyong Shire. The centres were manned by Kemcon staff who were able to continue to tell their story to their community and provide access to the facts about Kemcon. The centres were promoted through radio and press advertising and direct mail to all schools in Wyong Shire. Invitations were extended to visit the information centres and to request a plant tour.

Several videos were screened including one produced specifically for the centres with a message to the Wyong community from the Bayer managing director. The 'We do Kare' video was also adapted for community use.

A model of the Kemcon plant was displayed showing the safety features which had been constructed for environmental protection.

Photographic displays of the Kemcon plant compared conditions before and after Bayer's investment in environmental protection.

Products produced at the plant were displayed and also printed material including *KC News*, brochures, leaflets, comment cards and fact sheets.

A colouring competition for children attracted over 300 entries.

Wider community — January (year two and continuing)

Open-door policy

Kemcon adopted an open-door policy, inviting all Wyong media, residents, businesses and CCAC members to visit the plant for a formal tour and to receive answers to their questions.

Speeches

Kemcon executives and Bayer senior management, including the managing director, announced their availability to speak to community groups, service clubs or other interested organisations about Bayer/Kemcon's activities in Wyong.

Media coverage

A policy was adopted for Kemcon to obtain as much positive media coverage of its activities as possible.

Articles were not slanted as retaliatory or reactive but as quite independent of CCAC activities. A factual, proactive approach rather than an emotive approach was used.

Open day

Kemcon staff organised and conducted an 'open day' to which they invited families, local residents and neighbours to the site for a Sausage Sizzle and plant tours. Bayer supported the 'open day' with local advertising and some funding.

It was indicative of the significant improvement in staff attitudes that employees provided the food from their social club fund and gave their own time on a Saturday to host the day.

The advertising showed staff inviting residents to come and see the plant which had been positioned and described consistently as 'the safest, most environmentally sound operation of its kind in Australia'.

This gave the community an opportunity to see the plant at first hand and Kemcon employees were able to reinforce the message that: 'we have nothing to hide and we are proud of Kemcon'.

Budget

The total cost of the programme to year two was A$290,750, well within the budget figure. This was the budget under the direct control of the consultancy PPR. An additional advertising and legal budget related to the project was also committed by Bayer.

EVALUATION

The public relations activity in Wyong is now largely employee driven. Staff have been trained in dealing successfully with the media. They are 'locals' who can talk to locals in their own language and as a result are getting valuable media coverage.

The distribution of the staff newsletter *KC News* has been extended to include all target groups. Excerpts and stories are being used in local media features and included in the Bayer national magazines as an insert.

Recognition of the success of the programme has been endorsed by a formal letter from the International Director, Bayer Germany.

Open dialogue continues between the company, the local action groups and council through the monitoring committee.

At the end of year two, Greenpeace tried, unsuccessfully, to turn the Kemcon issue into one of national and even international proportions. The groundwork was in place for a better defence of the Bayer/chemical industry's position against attack and as a result it was possible to deflect any negative media attention.

As a result of the internal communication programme, employees will continue to play a pivotal role in the wider community communication programme. Generally, employees now feel comfortable about working at Kemcon and are proud of their company.

Involvement in the programme has assisted the personal development of some employees to the extent that several employees are now interested in pursuing a more active role in the community by standing for the local council.

The strong staff support for Kemcon has been evidenced on many occasions. For instance:

- breaking a state- and industry-wide union-organised strike when the staff knew that NBN3 (their regional television station) were due to do a story on the plant. Staff disregarded union instructions and manned the plant;
- mounting an 'open day' at the plant using social club funds to provide food and giving up their weekend leisure time;
- attending evening functions and meetings to assist the programme and attending Wyong Council meetings to monitor any matters relating to Kemcon;
- soliciting support from family and friends which resulted in over 1500 letters and possible submissions to Wyong Council in support of the Kemcon rezoning application and environmental impact statement. Several letters from staff and friends also appeared in the local press in support of Kemcon.

The programme has given and continues to give support to the many government and legal submissions which Bayer has had to make.

For ten years, Bayer had tried to establish a formulation plant in Australia. Bayer initially sought approvals for the establishment of a facility at Kurnell to replace the outdated plant at Botany. The company was under attack by action groups on many occasions during that period.

The purchase of an existing chemical plant in Wyong operating under the name of Kemcon was seen as an answer. Had the plant been attacked for its lack of operational and environmental safety in the first year of Bayer's ownership, it would almost certainly have been closed down. Bayer spent A$15 million in upgrading Kemcon which made it into something of a model for the chemical industry. It was incongruous, almost a travesty of justice, that the opposition to the Kemcon plant developed after this extensive upgrading.

The relocation of Kemcon would have been extremely difficult for Bayer and it would have jeopardised the continued operation and presence of Bayer in Australia. This would have also resulted in the loss of over 200 jobs of the local Wyong residents.

At the end of year two, Bayer presented a rezoning proposal to the Wyong Shire Council to allow them to build an additional small warehouse on an adjoining site. An EIS was reviewed by Wyong Council to re-evaluate the activities of Kemcon in Wyong and how they affected local residents, companies and the adjoining wetlands. The rezoning and the new development were agreed.

The PPR communication programmes gave Wyong Shire councillors, residents, neighbours and action groups the opportunity to hear the facts, see the operation, and evaluate the written material made available to them.

Bayer managing director, Peter Senne, wrote in *KC News* regarding the success of 'Neighbours' Day at Kemcon:

> We need the dialogue, not only in relation to acute issues like the EIS, the development application, and the question of how does the plant fit into the industrial and community activities of Wyong and the Central Coast, but in every aspect of our daily life. By talking to each other, many 'could be' problems will not even develop into real ones.

In year three, following two years of negotiation and open dialogue between Bayer and the government of the day, the Environment Minister at that time, Robert Webster, successfully proposed changes to state legislation which allowed for hazardous industries to operate in any industrial zone (State Environmental Planning Policy No 33). The influence of the local action group (CCAC) in the community markedly diminished which allowed Bayer to proceed with the development application (DA) under the terms of the policy. The DA was approved and extensions to the plant have now been completed and the name of the plant has been confidently changed to Bayer Kemcon.

CASE DISCUSSION

This case study has been included in the chapter dealing with the protection of the environment, but it could equally have been included under 'employee relations'. Carolyne Paris, Group Director of Professional Public Relations Pty Ltd of Sydney, is to be congratulated on the successful harnessing of employee power to support the company's fight for survival.

The careful initial research indicated the lines on which the programme should be planned and it is noteworthy that unstinted support was forthcoming from Bayer Australia when requested to back up local endeavours.

The current concern in Australia with environmental protection is in happy contrast to personal experience in the 1960s of a large power station in New South Wales belching forth clouds of toxic fumes over a neighbouring leisure and holiday area.

IPRA has published a charter on environmental communication which was adopted by the IPRA Council in November 1991 and which emphasises the contribution which public relations practitioners can make to environmental protection. This account of the Battle of Wyong indicates how sound public relations principles can help industry to protect its corporate objectives at the same time as safeguarding the local environment.

It is also very interesting to note how a comparatively small budget was involved because the active support of the employees was mobilised so effectively.

4

Employee Relations

Case 4.1 Communications 2000 at Rhône-Poulenc

BACKGROUND

A major and growing problem in industry, in the United Kingdom and in most other countries, is the need to improve internal communications. It is now generally accepted that effective and consistent communication between management and employees is essential to ensure a happy workforce and the successful operation of a plant or factory.

The question of communication is exacerbated when a company is subjected to a takeover by a foreign company. This was the situation at Research Triangle Park in North Carolina, USA where Rhône-Poulenc Ag Company (R-P Ag) is a US operation of Rhône-Poulenc S.A., the largest French chemical company.

The company recorded dynamic growth in the United States following a major acquisition in 1987. R-P Ag manufactures agricultural crop protection products and has 2600 employees at nine sites, plus field offices, with headquarters in Research Triangle Park. Sites vary from seven to 1400 employees.

The merging of corporate cultures and the parent company's French heritage left many employees with a need for a clearer understanding of the company's new culture and future. The situation was potentially unstable.

OVERALL OBJECTIVES OF THE PROGRAMME

The company had four clear objectives in planning a two-way communication programme which it called 'Communications 2000'. They were:

1. to create an environment where employees could be more creative and productive;
2. to develop a strong corporate culture based on accepted values;
3. to help management to be more responsive to employee needs; and
4. to be highly specific, budget conscious and to contribute in a tangible way to profitability.

RESEARCH

The purpose of the research was to establish benchmarks by combining a communication audit of the effectiveness of existing communication channels with a comprehensive look at employee opinions on job satisfaction issues such as the company's management style, culture and values and preparedness to meet any crisis.

Measurable research objectives

1. Communication audit:
   — to compare existing with desired sources of information;
   — to evaluate the credibility of sources;
   — to identify the information important to employees;
   — to measure the level of knowledge about company issues.
2. Employee-company issues:
   — to assess employee perceptions of community relations;
   — to evaluate R-P Ag culture and internal relationships;
   — to determine the awareness of company values.

Initial research

In January 1990, an in-depth communication survey was posted to all employees. The survey was designed to determine how employees perceive and relate to the company and to establish a benchmark for modifying existing communications or to develop new programmes to meet identified needs. The research was carried out by Dudley Research for the company and the basis of their research programme is given in Figure 8.

A good response rate was encouraged by the questionnaire being accompanied by a personal letter to each employee from the president of the company urging them to respond. The value of this approach was shown by an employee response rate of 41 per cent, a very high return for such a complicated questionnaire.

┌─────────────────── **DUDLEY RESEARCH** ───────────────────┐

RESEARCH STATEMENT:

To determine how key publics perceive & relate to
Rhône-Poulenc Ag Company; and, how this translates
behaviorally.

RESEARCH OBJECTIVES:

1. What are the best sources of information about R-P
   Ag, R-P Inc & R-P S.A.?

2. What is the level of believability & credibility in
   these information sources?

3. Identify the realm of information employees desire
   about each level of the company & the most
   preferred method for delivering this information.

4. Assess key publics' satisfaction with R-P Ag &
   their relationships with it.

5. Model/estimate response to a crisis issue.

6. Evaluate present state of Rhône-Poulenc Ag Co
   culture.

7. Determine awareness of company values.

8. Measure level of knowledge of company issues,
   values, vulnerabilities.

9. Determine whether or not the company "lives its
   values"; is what RP Ag is "known for" in fact what
   it "stands for"?

10. Verify relevant aspects of Jan '89 research.

└──┘

Figure 8 A statement of the agreed research methodology

The results revealed serious problems with employee morale and internal communications. Employees felt they were not receiving the information they wanted about the company; they did not know company values; and they felt managers were insensitive to their needs.

The research methodology used two innovative techniques: *semantic evaluation* to simplify the assimilation of qualitative data from many open-ended questions and *force-field analysis* of the results to aid in strategic planning.

PROGRAMME PLANNING AND EXECUTION

Based on the research findings, the plans for Communications 2000 included:

1. Improving internal information systems to better meet employee needs by:
   i) developing a new logo to give a dramatic and easily identifiable corporate message to all company publications;
   ii) revitalizing the company newsletter *AgCommunique* and making a distribution change by posting it to employee homes;
   iii) initiating *AgVisory* to help managers to be better conduits of information both from employees to senior management and vice versa;
   iv) designing a simple grid lay-out system for publications using desk top publishing equipment;
   v) developing an editorial plan for all publications to ensure they respond to the priority information needs identified by the survey;
   vi) developing a protocol book to ensure consistency of publications.
2. Two new interactive programmes were introduced:
   i) *'Lunch with ...'*
   At headquarters, a senior executive has lunch once a month with a cross-section of employees, followed by informal discussion.
   ii) *'La France et les Français'*
   This is a French culture programme held at headquarters to build bridges with their French parent company. The employee committee which planned this programme used considerable imagination in planning suitable events to capture employees' imagination.

Figure 9 shows the way in which the invitations to lunch are issued and Figure 10 is an example of the attendance at a typical lunch meeting. Employees are selected on a rotating basis from different work levels, including secretaries, middle management and technicians. Attendance is limited to 12 to allow maximum opportunity for active discussion. Each lunch has a chosen topic which is notified in advance so that attendees can prepare questions or comments. After the meeting, a summary of the questions and answers is prepared for each attendee to share with fellow employees either at departmental meetings, one-to-one or as hand-outs. This extends the value of the lunch meetings beyond the men and women who are invited. Additionally, reports of the sessions are featured in the employee newsletter to keep all employees informed.

3. Values
    The company focused on two activities to make company values better understood and applied by all employees:
    i) Using *AgCommunique* and *AgVisory* to discuss the values and present examples of employees 'living' the values in day-to-day operations.
    ii) Training that links values with communication skills.
4. Addressing human relations issues.
    The Executive Management Committee has initiated an experimental work week schedule and a modification of summer working hours.

EVALUATION OF COMMUNICATIONS 2000

- The company now has a detailed and reliable benchmark.
- Evaluation of employee communications. Readership studies measured the effectiveness of the revitalised *AgCommunique* and the newly established *AgVisory*. Follow-up research from a random sample of managers and employees indicated a more positive feeling about the publications. Both managers and employees said that *AgCommunique* now helped them to understand better the complex company history, its corporate values and its future direction and that their families also read it.
    Managers said that *AgVisory* gave them a better idea of what was going on in other departments of R-P Ag and gave them information they could share with staff and helped them to answer questions.

Bob Kattman

Congratulations on being selected to represent
your fellow employees at a

Lunch with . . .

Phil Nelson

General Manager-Southern Area Countries, Crop Protection Division

on

Monday, July 15

Conference Room 1318
from 12:45 to 2 p.m.

Please come prepared with questions that you
and your fellow employees have about our company or industry.
Please turn in this invitation for your free cafeteria
lunch on that day, bringing it to our meeting
room promptly.
If you have any questions or for any reason
cannot attend, please contact me at X 2850.

Michael Reichgut—Director, Corporate Affairs and Employee Communications

Figure 9 Example of an invitation to 'Lunch with ...'

"LUNCH with . . ." Program Attendees

September 7, 1990

Andre de Marco
Director—Rhone-Poulenc S.A.
Group Communications

Commercial Area:	**Irwin Fishkin**	
		Communications
	Jerry Garnett	
		Communications
Finance/MIS:	**Tom Hunter**	
		Site Services
	Sandra de Montbrun	
		MIS
Operations:	**Joel Leeper**	
		Materials & Distribution
Human Resources:	**Tomas Perez**	
		Human Resources
Administration/Other:	**Jeanne McPherson**	**Strategic**
	Business Development	
Research & Development	**Jeff Charles**	
		Toxicology
	Danielle Larochelle	
	Product Q/A & Tech Service	
	Russ Outcalt	
		Discovery Research
	Sue Singawacha	
		Metabolism
Environmental, Regulatory & Public Affairs:	**Elizabeth Newby**	**Corporate Affairs**
Moderator:	**Jim Haskins**	**Mgr. Communications**
Monitor:	**Erica Upton**	**Communications Intern**

Figure 10 The mixture of Program Attendees

- Interactive programmes.
  i) *La France et les Français*
     These events, presented by volunteers, draw 'standing room only' crowds and are eagerly attended by spouses and some members of the community.
  ii) *'Lunch with ...'*
     Initially designed for senior executives of R-P Ag based in the United States, this programme is now used to help bridge the cultural gulf between French executives and American employees.
     Attendee feedback forms are used to evaluate each session. On a scale of 0 to 5, meetings have averaged 4 +.
- Human relations issues.
  A survey on the modification of summer working hours gave 85 per cent approval. The compressed work week also received an 85 per cent satisfaction level.

A MANAGEMENT ASSESSMENT

The following extracts from a report by Rhône-Poulenc's top management group describes their opinion of the many programmes which were introduced as a result of needs identified in the employee survey.

Executive Management Committee (EMC) Programme for the future

Many employees who responded to our communications survey used it as a way to share with us their thoughts and feelings on a variety of topics beyond communications. They took the opportunity to use it as a way to communicate directly with management – something they said they felt they have generally not been able to do.

The data and voluntary comments should be used as a guide for the direction senior management and the organisation now takes to improve internal relations. The reason for pursuing a particular agenda should be based on the research or management will appear as unresponsive to the employees. This does not mean that everything must be changed just because it has been requested. It is prudent to respond to the major issues with change where appropriate and with explanations when not.

The EMC stated it was important to consider that:

- good internal relationships are critical to making safety improvements, productivity gains, increased innovation and the ability to overcome practically every other internal dilemma;
- employees and communities are influenced not only by our performance and actions, but also by how well we identify and individualise communications to their specific needs;
- a free flow of information, up and down the organisation, will help keep the company competitive;
- it is critical for senior management to empower people by pushing not only decision-making, but communication down the organisation. A goal for progressive and successful companies will be to find ways to keep employees motivated and supportive.

Other actions taken by the EMC

- The EMC group recognised a high level of employee interest in modifying summer working hours. A task force of employees from across the site was commissioned to study and evaluate options. As a result, a new trial schedule allowing employees to be off a half-day per week was implemented.
- An Employee Assistance Programme was initiated. In this programme, a counsellor is designated who is located within driving distance of each site. All employees can utilise this programme to receive professional help on problems related to work, family, financial, chemical abuse, and any other issues adversely affecting them or members of their families. This counselling is free of charge until such time that a referral is made to a specialised resource.
- An Employee Appreciation Day was introduced. This additional day off was granted to recognise the contributions of all employees to the recent success of the company.
- Senior management committed, and demonstrated by their actions, words and programmes that they would neither support nor allow situations that promote 'we-they' attitudes within the company.
- A committee recommended the type of Total Management programme that would be most effective in promoting teamwork, partnership and participation.
- Corporate and divisional training programmes had always been sponsored for employees. A review of the programmes ensured that these are meeting the needs of employees.

- To meet requests from employees, a suggestions scheme was introduced.

A general report on management's reaction to the Survey Research and their proposals for action was published in *AgCommunique* for the information of all employees.

CASE DISCUSSION

This case study is notable for the way in which, having identified the potential instability of the situation, the company engaged a professional market research organisation to carry out a comprehensive communication audit, including a detailed questionnaire.

Sometimes a company thinks that this exploratory action is all that is necessary. Credit is due to Rhône-Poulenc for accepting the results of the research and taking immediate steps to introduce all its recommendations. Even the dissatisfaction expressed with certain aspects of remuneration and working conditions was faced and appropriate steps taken to try to ameliorate these complaints.

It is interesting to note how the difference in culture between the French headquarters and the American subsidiary was used creatively to bring a new stimulus to employees who wished to take an interest in matters other than merely earning a living.

Internal programmes of public relations will not automatically avoid all conflicts and problems but it is certain that the positive steps taken by the Rhône-Poulenc management in North Carolina will have had a very beneficial influence on the company's fortunes.

Case 4.2 An employee communication plan

BACKGROUND

The J I Case Company, with headquarters in Racine, Wisconsin, USA, is a major world-wide producer of farm and construction equipment. The Parts and Components Division of the company (PAC) employs about 4500 people, mostly based in Racine, and the remainder at parts depots throughout North America and Europe.

Late in 1988, the public relations consultancy Communication Concepts Unlimited (CCU) was asked by the new executive vice-president of the division to suggest a communication plan to energise his division towards increased productivity, quality and service.

RESEARCH

CCU was formed in 1983 and has worked for J I Case since its formation. The company brought to the PAC assignment an in-depth knowledge of the company culture, organisational structure and existing communication channels.

CCU began the assignment by working closely with the vice-president to establish positive goals and objectives and to coordinate a comprehensive, unified programme. The agreed objectives were:

1. to communicate the division's new name to employees and to build up employee morale;
2. to communicate and support the notion of continuous improvement within all segments of the organisation;
3. to support the process of enhancing customer awareness among all the employees.

The theme of the plan was given a memorable title 'Together we can' which formed the core of each element of the programme.

Existing communication programmes within the different sections of the company were examined and assessed for effectiveness in case they could suggest ways of developing the

PAC communication programme. It was clear that there were few direct vehicles for management and employees to communicate with each other. It was decided that the PAC Division needed an identity programme to solidify employee morale and to motivate employees to take responsibility for their own jobs.

PLANNING

The communication programme which was agreed with the management of PAC had four main facets:

1. Introduction of employees to the 'Together we can' theme.
2. Development of a newsletter, directory and videos.
3. Special programmes.
4. Communicating with external audiences.

The primary audiences were employees, sales staff and the external community.

IMPLEMENTATION

1. The employees were introduced to the new scheme in dramatic fashion. When PAC employees returned from their Christmas break in January 1989, they were greeted with a brass band, banners strung throughout the offices and manufacturing plants, and posters highlighting the 'Together we can' theme. Members of management accompanied the band and distributed leaflets describing the objectives and goals of the PAC division.

   The 'Together we can' spirit was extended to outlying locations with special 'care packages' that included banners, cards and posters for their own launch of the programme. Visits by senior management were conducted throughout North America and Europe at various times throughout the year.

   Executive management met groups of employees in the weeks that followed the introduction of the programme to explain in greater detail the goals of the division and to emphasise their genuine commitment to work together. A series of quarterly meetings was initiated to provide continuing communication. Several units within the division also held 'skip level' meetings to foster greater dialogue within various segments of the operations, particularly in manufacturing. CCU wrote, produced and distributed all materials.

2. An employee newsletter was initiated, entitled *Excellence*. It was written by CCU and produced each month on a Macintosh desktop publishing system to contain costs and to allow greater production flexibility.

   In addition to regular features, PAC management used the newsletter to communicate important financial news in a special four-page mid-year issue and to boost morale with an all photo issue produced following the employee outdoor 'PACnic' celebration. The first employee directory was compiled to help employees to be able to communicate more effectively within the division. It was designed to list names and telephone numbers and information about how the division was organised and structured.

   Two videos were produced for employees. The first video featured the executive vice-president on the subject of excellence and quality control. The second video, 'Heroism' was a 10-minute presentation which highlighted achievements of employees. It focused on Case people as the heroes who make a positive contribution to group and corporate performance through hard work, customer focus and a renewed dedication to the basic principles of quality.

   The core of this video highlighted employees photographed at Group locations world-wide. The video's debut was at the Group's Parts Trade Fair held in Kansas City for Case farm and construction equipment dealers. A special dealer module, added to the video, underscored the importance of dealer support and follow through. This incorporated images of dealers taken at the conference. This 'Heroism' video was also used in 1989 and 1990 at management and employee presentations.

3. The main special programmes which were introduced were 'Open House' and the 'PACnic' employee summer gathering.

   A plant open house was organised for the autumn of 1989 to demonstrate the innovation and dedication of PAC employees. CCU wrote and produced a video in conjunction with the United Auto Workers Union about Case workers. It featured seven employees talking about their work and ambitions. One thousand copies were distributed to employees and management and 10,000 employees and guests viewed the video at the open house.

   In conjunction with the open house, the PAC Transmission Plant in Racine requested that a brochure be written, designed and printed at short notice. The resultant four-colour, six-page, fold out brochure was used at the open house and is now given to visitors who tour the plant.

In August 1989, the first employee 'PACnic' summer gathering was held for employees and their families. Food, soft drinks, games and fun were the order of the day. A special PACnic logo signalled the event and was emblazoned on everything from signs and balloons to the mugs in the refreshment tent. A special edition of the company newsletter, filled with photographs of employees was published following the event. An employee-produced video of the event was edited and made available for later enjoyment.

4. Communicating with external audiences included a 'Share the vision' meeting for suppliers and agents and the production of a PAC 1990 calendar. Media relations were also stepped up.

The 'Share the vision' meeting was held in the spring of 1989 by PAC for suppliers and agents. The sessions, held first at the company's engineering and test centre, and later at other locations, was organised under the theme 'Together we can – share the vision'. The events included touring company locations and meeting senior management.

During 1989, preparations were made for producing a four-colour PAC 1990 calendar, to be distributed to PAC suppliers and customers around the world. The focus of the calendar was PAC employees from each depot world-wide. To enhance employee participation, local units were encouraged to choose settings that would typify their city, region or country. Locations selected included Independence Hall in Philadelphia, the marina at San Leandre, a street scene in Heidelberg, an ancient castle in Yorkshire and a Saskatchewan grain elevator.

Throughout the year, business press contacts were made and media releases were distributed to enhance communication about group activities within the communities where the group's plants and depots operate.

EVALUATION

Success of employee communication programmes can be evaluated in various ways. Does management like it? Has it improved employee morale? Has employee productivity improved? By all these measurements, the PAC communication plan was successful. Management not only implemented all major aspects of the plan, but was committed to continuing the programme and expanding it.

Employee morale improved as witnessed by the enthusiastic response to the PACnic event, the plant open house, and the dealer and other meetings.

Productivity also improved. Sales for the PAC division increased by 14 per cent during the year. The PAC division became recognised as the leading edge of Case performance, both from a profit standpoint and in terms of cohesive, team-approach perspectives.

The PAC division has become highly regarded as a unit where performance is recognised, job enrichment is encouraged and quality of life and quality of work and product are priorities.

CASE DISCUSSION

It is interesting to compare this report with Case 4.1 which describes the employee relations programme initiated at Rhône-Poulenc. In both cases, the management believed that steps could be taken to improve internal communication and to enhance job satisfaction that would have beneficial results for the employees and also improve productivity and profitability.

It is generally accepted that employee public relations is likely to be the most rapidly developing aspect of the whole public relations spectrum. Traditionally, industry in most countries has not been particularly good at communicating with employees. There is ample evidence, however, that the 'grapevine' is a dangerous and pernicious threat in industrial relations. This danger can only be fought successfully by a well-planned and efficient programme of internal communication.

The two case studies in this chapter dealing with employee relations show a fairly uniform approach to the challenge of ensuring that employees are 'human resources' which both need and deserve intelligent and enlightened consideration.

It is perhaps relevant to mention here the seven conditions which have become accepted as important for harmony in the workplace. These are:

1. Full and truthful information, flowing freely up, down and sideways.
2. Trust and confidence between employer and employees.
3. Healthy and safe working conditions.
4. Fair and equitable remuneration.
5. Continuity of work without conflict.
6. Work satisfaction, most of the time.
7. Pride in the organisation and optimism for its future.

Judged by these criteria, the two companies described in this chapter have taken the right approach to the delicate problem of communicating with employees.

5

Community Relations

Case 5.1 IMPACT India and the Magic Train

BACKGROUND

In November 1981, a seminar at Leeds Castle, England brought together an international group of scientists, health specialists and politicians of world standing under the chairmanship of Lord Home. The meeting finished with the adoption of the Leeds Castle Declaration: 'Avoidable disability is a prime cause of economic waste and human deprivation in all countries, industrialized and developing. This loss can be reduced rapidly'.

In order to translate the recommendations into action, IMPACT was created. It represents a unique initiative by bringing together the resources of the United Nations with the vigour of private enterprise and the expertise of governments with the dedication of community self-help.

India was chosen to be the site of the global launch of the IMPACT initiative because it had the capacity to tackle disability prevention and had developed a number of low-cost technologies useful in preventing disabilities. The major thrust of the IMPACT India initiative was to be on the level of primary health care: prevention of diseases like poliomyelitis, goitre, blindness and serious infections. About two million people become disabled in India each year.

The success achieved by IMPACT India in Madras, Bombay and elsewhere was the result of coordinating available resources in the public and private sectors into a working whole. Without this, the various inputs would have remained disjointed and isolated. For example, Voltas Limited, India's largest marketing, engineering and manufacturing enterprise, has donated the skills of its senior management, communications and technical professionals to firmly establish IMPACT in India. IMPACT acts as a catalyst, using the strengths of the business houses to work with the government on mass welfare programmes. The project is considered to be an excellent model for the entire developing world.

PLANNING

IMPACT India's role was:

1. communicating with agencies, both governmental and non-governmental, to secure resources;
2. communicating with the government to get sanctions and support;
3. communicating awareness in the beneficiaries in order to create demand.

Folk media is popular in India. It has been a form of public communication through the ages and continues to be one of the most important media for development and social change. For example, IMPACT India used this effectively to communicate the need for immunisation. Through street plays and puppetry, the message of immunisation was taken into the streets and community centres. College students and volunteers performed street plays that spread health education which reinforced opinions that made immunisation socially acceptable.

IMPACT India has used communication to harness existing resources and has exerted a salutary influence on established agencies and organisations. As a government and UN promoted initiative backed by prominent leaders of the Indian business community, it has lent legitimacy to its developmental objectives and to the people and organisations involved.

IMPLEMENTATION

Communication has been the basis of success. IMPACT India is an inspiration to action, a call to identify talent and to harness it in the best interests of the community. Voltas believes that since the corporate sector serves the vast majority of India's population, corporate bodies who are sound financially, professionally and resource-wise are the best support that ought to be extended to the government machinery to help in realising its objectives.

Voltas has concentrated its support in the field of health care to reach out to 70 million disabled people through IMPACT India. Its latest programme has been the production of a Lifeline Express (or

'The Magic Train of India' according to *Newsweek* of 12 October, 1992). The railway system of India has 65,000 km of track, with 7000 sidings for convenient parking. So the Lifeline Express (*Jeevan Rekha*) was conceived to carry medical care and hospital services to wherever it was needed.

The train consists of three remodelled railway coaches. The key coach houses the operation theatre, with three adjustable operating tables and other sophisticated medical equipment, a sterilising room, a diagnostic centre with large supplies of drugs and antibiotics, and a lying-in ward with 12 beds for post-operative care. All the equipment has been modified to withstand the rigours of long journeys. The second coach contains the living quarters for the surgeons, medical and para-medical staff and stores, while the third coach holds the kitchen, two generators and living space for the train staff.

All the 26–30 doctors and nurses are volunteers. The train usually stops in one spot for six weeks. The staff concentrate on common medical problems such as cataracts, mid-ear deafness or polio – all of which can be alleviated with relatively simple surgery. The work-load is heavy: some ophthalmic surgeons have performed as many as 70 cataract operations in a single day aboard the train. A typical programme at a six-week stop is: 1000 orthopaedic cases, 800 ophthalmic operations or treatments, and 500 hearing loss cases. The cost of preparing and equipping the train was £200,000 and the whole operation has been made possible by cooperation between Voltas Ltd, Indian Railways, some charitable organisations and a number of large corporate bodies who have contributed liberally to the funds. Voltas Ltd made available the services of three of its senior executives to direct the project with a high level of professionalism with their technical, communication and administrative skills.

The idea of the travelling train was conceived by Mrs Zelma Lazarus, general manager of corporate relations at Voltas Ltd, who has acted as the director of IMPACT India. Previously she has been loaned by the company to act as regional consultant to United Nations development programmes. This willingness by Voltas Ltd to second Mrs Lazarus for vital development work is an excellent example of community relations.

CASE DISCUSSION

The involvement of a leading Indian public relations practitioner in development projects of such national importance is quite appropriate as the techniques and strategies involved are similar to those required for success in typical public relations programmes. What is more remarkable, perhaps, is the willingness of a major Indian company to second a senior executive to this work on such a long-term commitment. The corporate image of Voltas Ltd in India must have been enhanced greatly by the company's readiness to be involved and to take a leading part in community projects of such magnitude.

Public relations for a large organisation goes much further than media relations or marketing and the story of IMPACT India and the magic train is an outstanding example of corporate social responsibility.

Case 5.2 Painting the community

BACKGROUND

The 'Dulux Community Projects Scheme' has been operating since 1980. It has achieved its purpose of bringing ICI Paints into direct contact with many sections of the community and has given the company a human face while maintaining its position as the brand leader in paint. The scheme has been promoted entirely by public relations without any advertising support.

RESEARCH

In the late 1970s, ICI Paints became concerned that their image among customers was becoming too 'high tech'. Research in the UK undertaken to establish the public's attitude to ICI Paints' Dulux brand showed that while consumers credited ICI with making the best paint, they regarded Dulux as being removed from everyday life. 'Aloof' and 'too scientific' were the adjectives most commonly used when describing the brand. Dulux conjured up visions of men in white coats and laboratories where correct formulae were produced. The brand did not convey the warmth, approachability and friendliness which ICI felt was essential if they were to be able to encourage the use of Dulux in the home.

In view of these research findings, it was considered essential to make consumers more comfortable with the Dulux brand. This had to be achieved, however, without losing the positive aspects of being brand leader in the UK retail paint sector and widely perceived as the very best quality paint.

A public relations consultancy, Welbeck Golin/Harris, was briefed to devise a campaign which would change consumer attitudes towards the Dulux brand. The stated objectives were:

1. to create a programme which would clearly associate Dulux with caring, warmth, friendliness and approachability;
2. to continue to associate the brand with the technical excellence of ICI Paints, but to offer this as a means of reassurance rather than intimidation;

3. to underline the brand's position as the market leader;
4. to make direct contact with consumers as well as via the media.

PLANNING

In planning the campaign, it was decided that it was necessary to create a public relations programme which would reflect the new brand values and be of social significance in line with ICI's responsibility as the brand leader.

It was agreed that the activity should operate at grassroots level, involving all sectors of the community so that its media appeal would reach the broad spectrum of current and potential paint users. Moreover, the effect of the programme would be long-term and the altered public perception of the brand would be sustained.

The programme which was developed to meet the demands of the brief was the Dulux Community Projects Awards Scheme, which was launched in 1980 and is still continuing to meet ICI's objectives by emphasising the company's commitment to the community, and has helped to change public attitude to the brand. The concept was for ICI Paints to create a scheme whereby they would donate large quantities of Dulux paint to suitable voluntary groups and charities throughout the United Kingdom. Any group could apply, providing the work they planned using the paint for would benefit the community.

The country was divided into five regions and an independent panel of judges, drawn from the voluntary sector, was appointed. This scheme ensured that media coverage would be generated throughout the country and that Dulux would be portrayed as the generous patron of the scheme, rather than a manufacturer with a vested interest.

IMPLEMENTATION

The scheme was launched in Spring 1980 with a reception attended by national press, consumer interest magazines, radio and television, and London-based news agencies who syndicated the story to regional publications. In addition, a direct mail campaign was undertaken to all UK-based national charitable and voluntary organisations, inviting them to pass on the information to their regional members.

Posters and application forms were produced and distributed widely through libraries and Citizens' Advice Bureaux, together with current Dulux colour cards. All successful applicants could choose any paint from the current Dulux retail range, rather than be forced to accept old or discontinued lines.

Administration of the scheme is handled by Welbeck Golin/ Harris who have a part of their offices devoted to The Dulux Community Projects Office. All applications are studied here and summarised before being passed to the independent panel of judges for assessment. Awards are made on an annual basis.

A special selection category has been added to the scheme. Those groups judged by the panel of judges to be most deserving because of the creativity of their project, and its value to the community, are given a special cash award. This generates further media coverage and provides good 'before' and 'after' photography.

Typical winners

A feature of the scheme over the years has been the amazing variety of schemes which have applied for paint to be supplied. The following are a few examples of schemes which were successful in their applications and completed the approved schemes:

1. The John Edward Cope Trust at Nuneaton used its donation of paint to redecorate three buildings which house 15 homeless people.
2. Faversham Age Concern centre was repainted by eight volunteers from Faversham Town Football Club.
3. A mural painted on the boundary wall of their resource centre at Osmonthorpe Lane, Leeds. The mural, painted by disabled people, depicts a variety of subjects, from the Dulux sheepdog to Van Gogh type sunflowers.
4. Dedicated members of the Coventry Steam Railway restored a 97-year-old signal box to its former glory.
5. Peterborough Arts Council used their gift of paint to redecorate a number of different projects in the town catering for youth and the disabled.
6. The Alternative Arts Commission at Amersham organises groups of young people, some of whom have been convicted for illegal graffiti, to paint murals on appropriate walls of buildings in the area. This has the dual purpose of brightening up the areas and preventing them being used again for graffiti.
7. Blacon adventure playground was transformed into a huge rainforest designed by playground workers and children.
8. The Downend Folk House in Bristol was completely repainted

inside and outside. In charge of the painters, all retired men, was 83-year-old ex-chairman, Horace Adams.

9.   At Gloucester, youngsters from the White City Adventure Playground Association painted a colourful mural on their new playhut.

These examples, taken at random from a vast library of reports of successful schemes, shows how the gifts of paint help a wide variety of projects. Needless to say, the local media give wide coverage to all these newsworthy stories.

The excellent publicity that the Dulux scheme receives in the local and regional press is supplemented by many radio reports and interviews with jubilant winners.

EVALUATION

The statistics illustrate the success of the scheme. On average, more than 10,000 charities and voluntary groups apply for free paint each year. During the 12 years of the programme, over 4500 organisations have completed projects helped by the distribution of £500,000 worth of free paint. The significance of this programme is enhanced by the fact that apart from the winners each year there are many other applicants who hope to apply again the following year.

Media coverage continues annually in the national and regional press and in the radio and broadcast media. The company considers that by regularly involving charities and voluntary groups, it is associating the brand with an image of caring, warmth and friendliness which has helped Dulux remain the brand leader. Qualitative research has confirmed this view.

CASE DISCUSSION

Many experts, within both public relations and management, consider that it is essential to come up continually with new ideas for programmes and would advise against repeating schemes, however creative and successful they prove to be.

This constant search for new ideas is praiseworthy but both this ICI Dulux case study and the report of the Santam's Child Art project, reported in Case 9.2, emphasise that there can be exceptions to this general rule.

When a company, acting on advice from its public relations

advisers, implements a scheme that proves to be very successful, both for the people who participate and the resulting wide media coverage, there does not seem to be any valid reason for curtailing its life-span simply in the interest of novelty. This is particularly true of this Dulux story which, by its very nature, rejuvenates itself each year as the new competition is announced and awards made.

Another good aspect of this case study is that the award itself relates quite specifically to the product. The South African insurance company Santam cannot match this as it could hardly give away free policies. Both ICI and Santam, however, appeal through their programmes to a very wide range of people and organisations and to a wide age range. This breadth of appeal is true of ICI directly and Santam through parents, grandparents and relations of the budding artists and designers.

While everybody would agree that it is a 'good' thing to pursue an active policy of community relations, some sceptics query whether or not there is any direct benefit to the company as a result of the resources expended on this kind of activity.

Lord Laing of Dunphail, when chairman of United Biscuits, initiated the Per Cent Club to which about 500 leading British companies belong. Member companies pledge to donate to the community one per cent of profits before tax. At their annual general meeting (March 1992), HRH The Prince of Wales, president of Business in the Community (BITC) emphasised that industry's help to the community should not just be a question of cash. He said that contribution in terms of equipment, food, employee time and seconded personnel could make an enormous difference. It is necessary to persuade people that business actually does have a human face, it does care and can contribute an enormous amount of value.

The Prince's contribution was supported by a report at the meeting by Bain and Company, management consultants, which revealed that companies with formal board-level policies for the community appeared significantly more successful in this field than firms with an informal policy or none at all. As regards actual business benefits, the report stated that those most commonly cited related to employee morale, demonstrating care and support as an employer, and helping staff development and recruitment.

Case 5.3 Child Survival Programme in the Philippines

BACKGROUND

The United Nations Children's Emergency Fund (UNICEF) conceived and implemented a Child Survival Programme to help deprived children in the worst affected areas of the world.

Johnson & Johnson (J & J), the leading US corporation marketing a wide variety of consumer, pharmaceutical and professional health care products in 150 countries, was receptive to UNICEF's appeal for grants to fund this programme, and in 1987 J & J had awarded three-year grants for use in Zambia, Zimbabwe and Guatemala.

In the Philippines, the company has been represented by Johnson & Johnson (Philippines) Inc. since 1956 and the line of J & J baby products has been very popular with Philippine families.

In early 1990, J & J (Philippines) was looking for a project that would make a significant and positive impact on the public, particularly on mothers and children who are the main consumers of J & J products, as well as on the government and the Department of Health (DOH) which supervised the health sector in which J & J was most involved.

Coincidentally, UNICEF had presented at that time a further proposal to J & J for a grant to fund a Child Survival Programme in the Philippines during the period 1990–91, on similar lines to the previous schemes in other countries. J & J (Philippines) strongly recommended approval of the UNICEF proposal, seeing it as just the high impact project it was looking for.

The threat to health

In 1984–95, the Philippine economy contracted to its 1975 level and the impact of the economic downturn was wide ranging and far reaching. Hardest hit were the children of farmers and urban poor who constituted over three-quarters of the country's then population of 56 million. Poverty-stricken families increased in numbers from 49 per cent in 1971 to 59 per cent in 1985. By 1987, almost 6 million families did not have the basic necessities of life. As a result, the overall health of the nation deteriorated.

The proposed J & J assistance would form part of the overall Child Survival Programme developed and being implemented by the Department of Health with the assistance of UNICEF and donor countries such as the United States, Canada, Australia and others.

The first objective of the DOH programme was to reduce the rate of infant mortality in the Philippines from 52.8 per thousand, the highest in the Asia Pacific region, to 47.8 by 1992. It also sought to bring down the rate of maternal deaths from 0.9 per thousand to 0.7 per thousand during the same period. The programme aimed to accomplish these objectives through community participation, health worker training, community health eduction and infant growth monitoring and promotion of basic supplies and equipment.

With the assistance of UNICEF and the donor countries, the Philippine government expanded its programme in 1988. The expansion was aimed at integrating maternal and child health by sharpening key programmes with direct impact on child survival by applying the Under-Six Clinic approach as the integrating mechanism for the delivery of services.

UNICEF's assistance was directed towards strengthening the existing programmes and services to children and mothers in disadvantaged communities. The specific UNICEF role in the Philippine Child Survival programme was to provide technical assistance in planning, monitoring implementation, training and the provision of supplies, equipment, delivery kits and communications equipment to Philippine government health agencies.

UNICEF would coordinate the use of the J & J grant to the Philippines, while the programme proper would be implemented by the Department of Health and its city, provincial, municipal and village health workers.

PLANNING

A contribution equivalent to $390,000 to UNICEF's budget for 1990–91 was recommended by J & J (Philippines) and approved by the US parent company.

The incidence of infant and maternal mortality was highest in geographically and culturally isolated areas as well as in poor urban areas. UNICEF identified 25 provinces and ten cities as high priority in requiring assistance in 1990–91.

Of the 25 provinces, seven were considered as critical and were receiving help from the DOH and other sponsors or organisations. The other 18 provinces, however, also needed urgent assistance and it was in those areas that J & J (Philippines) decided to concentrate its efforts in support of UNICEF. The production and dissemination of printed materials would maximise the benefits of the assistance. The printed materials would include:

1. growth monitoring charts, given to mothers by nurses at under-five clinics and other health facilities to track a baby's weight and health problems and to guide the mother in seeking medical help;
2. home-based mother records, given to mothers by midwives at health facilities to record the health history and condition of mothers-to-be and to guide them in seeking medical assistance in advance of actual need;
3. *Facts for Life Handbook*, a new publication, in comic format, to guide mothers on various health and related issues such as family planning, breast feeding, etc;
4. promotional handouts, in flyer form, to inform mothers on vital health matters affecting their babies such as growth monitoring, oral dehydration, breast feeding and immunisation.

A comprehensive public relations programme was prepared by Perceptions Inc of Manila. This plan included a national launching and press conference, the production of a special exhibit, the holding of seminars, and the issue of press and photo releases describing the grant and the programme.

IMPLEMENTATION

The management of Johnson & Johnson (Philippines) was actively involved throughout the execution of the project. They reviewed programme objectives, strategies and plans and provided management advice when required. They assisted in the preparation of the various publications to improve readability, layout and translation where necessary. The management provided advice regarding purchasing economics to eliminate waste and maximise the use of funds. They visited and monitored progress in the field on a quarterly basis. Lastly, they provided quality improvement process instruction to the UNICEF personnel.

The launching of the J & J grant was held at the Manila Hotel on 4 December 1990, with top officials from UNICEF, DOH and J & J (Philippines) in attendance. Members of the media were invited as it was intended that the launch should include a press conference. A special exhibit describing the Child Survival Programme and J & J's participation had been prepared and was displayed during the event.

Santiago Robles, senior vice president of J & J, announced the grant on behalf of J & J (Philippines) as the president, Godofredo Rodrigues, was abroad at the time. Robles expressed his belief that helping to meet the community needs was fundamental to the responsible way in which J & J conducted its business. He pointed out that his company believed that the cause of child survival was very urgent in the Philippines. Through this grant, J & J hoped to be able to make a significant contribution towards improving maternal care and reducing infant mortality in the country.

Both UNICEF Programme Coordinator, David Mason, and DOH Assistant Secretary, Dr Andrez Galvez, in their remarks at the launch, complimented J & J for its concern for the welfare of the mothers and children of the Philippines.

Nationwide seminars

Seminars were subsequently held in different parts of the country to brief and train DOH workers from various provinces and to give them the communication materials for distribution in their respective areas. Mr Robles attended and addressed several of these seminars, again highlighting J & J's involvement. The exhibit which had been displayed at the launch was shown during the seminars thus gaining further visibility for the company and its products. The exhibit was also displayed in the lobby at company headquarters in Paranaque, where it was seen by staff and visitors to the company.

To create further awareness about the programme among its various publics, J & J used UNICEF cards for its corporate Christmas cards in December 1990. These cards contained an insert describing the company's involvement in the Child Survival Programme.

Summary

Over the three-year period 1990–92, the J & J grant was used in the production of information, education and communication materials for the use of front-line health workers and mothers in the 18 high priority provinces. By the end of the three-year period, 2.3 million pieces of information material had been produced and distributed to about 1.2 million mothers each year. This is about 35 per cent of pregnant and lactating mothers on a national basis.

EVALUATION

The programme generated extensive favourable publicity for Johnson & Johnson (Philippines) throughout the media and also increased the public awareness of Johnson's baby products in a credible and dignified health-related manner. It undoubtedly increased awareness and goodwill towards J & J among mothers who would be unlikely to see J & J's advertisements. The publications of the Child Survival Programme were projected to reach 1.2 million mothers.

The programme also increased awareness and goodwill for J & J among government officials, especially those in the DOH, and health workers and medical professionals.

CASE DISCUSSION

This report is another example of the growing importance which large companies attach to corporate social responsibility. Helping the community is not altruism but rather enlightened self-interest. It is, however, the community which benefits. The company also gains, for there are obvious advantages in operating in a friendly environment.

The programme was planned and carried out successfully by Rene E Nieva, President of Perceptions Inc of Manila, working closely with Santiago Robles, senior vice president of Johnson & Johnson (Philippines).

Perceptions have been working as public relations counsellors for J & J since 1990. In 1994, Perceptions implemented another programme for J & J which was in some respects a logical continuation of the Child Survival Programme.

The Integrated Midwives Association of the Philippines (IMAP) and the Philippine Public Health Association (PPHA) invited Perceptions to produce a suitable programme for the awards to the 'Outstanding Midwives of the Philippines'. Rene Nieva persuaded J & J to sponsor this new award scheme which would recognise the important contribution that midwives make to the community. J & J responded favourably, so once again Rene Nieva worked closely with Santiago Robles who was now retired but in charge of the company's Philanthropic Contributions Programme.

This midwives awards scheme was so successful that it is being continued with J & J support. But that is another case history.

Case 5.4 People who care

BACKGROUND

The Co-operative Wholesale Society (CWS) is the major supplier of goods and services to Britain's largest retailer, the Co-operative movement. The Co-op is a huge organisation as the following statistics will indicate:

- The Co-op is Britain's biggest retailer, with nearly 5000 stores, ranging from small convenience shops to giant superstores.
- Co-op stores account for £7000 million worth of sales annually.
- The Co-op serves the consumer from farm to table. It is Britain's biggest farmer with 40,000 acres and is one of Europe's largest food manufacturing concerns, with 12 factories in the United Kingdom.
- The Co-op employs two Masters of Wine to advise on its extensive range of own-label wines.
- There are nearly 3000 products in the Co-op own brand range, including one of Britain's biggest selling teas − Co-op 99.

RESEARCH

Like other large organisations, the CWS carries out an extensive public relations programme which plays a prominent part in the successful operation of its many and varied interests.

The corporate statement of the Co-op is 'People who care' but research has shown that this theme is not adequately appreciated at the local level in many towns.

PLANNING

The objective of this particular public relations programme was to create a local community platform which would provide tangible evidence of the Co-op's caring philosophy as reflected in its corporate statement. Thus the main objective of the public relations programme developed for the CWS by Countrywide Communications (London) Ltd was to identify the Co-op as a modern retailer in tune with contemporary issues, communicating community concerns and issues and at the same time creating strong media opportunities.

Specially commissioned research sought to identify what children aged between 9 and 11 years of age regard as anti-social behaviour. A sample of 618 children was taken from urban and rural schools in north-west and south-east England and from Scotland. The questionnaire used was developed with the help of a children's panel, inviting the children to rank a number of statements concerning anti-social behaviour such as drink-driving, drug taking and racism. Children taking part in the research programme were asked to contribute essays and to draw posters depicting their anti-social concerns.

Professor Ronald Davis, consulting educational psychologist and a member of the National Curriculum Committee dealing with citizenship, was appointed to give extra depth to the survey through contributing to the development of the questionnaire.

The results of the survey were incorporated into a report entitled *'Anti-social — who cares?'*. Excerpts from children's essays and some of their drawings were used to illustrate the report. Preview copies of the report were mailed to a comprehensive list of opinion formers in order to gain endorsement of the research project and quotes for inclusion in subsequent press releases. Recipients of the report included chief constables of regional police forces, whose comments provided strong news angles for issue to the local press, particularly concerning the issue of drink-driving. A drawing depicting a child surrounded by anti-social images was commissioned for distribution with the press information.

A series of local radio interviews was arranged, featuring Professor Davis. During the recording session, an interview request came through from the Jimmy Young Show resulting in a five-minute live interview with Professor Davis.

Regional press competitions were placed to support in-store activity with the Co-op Community Challenge promotion, a board game offered to shoppers in return for proof of purchase and till receipts.

EVALUATION

A campaign of this nature requires endorsement by many authorities if it is to be taken seriously in the community and in the schools. This programme received enthusiastic endorsement from the following third parties and opinion formers:

- The Minister of Roads, Christopher Choat.
- The Association of Chief Police Officers, New Scotland Yard, and Police Constabularies representing Norfolk, Central Scotland, Warwickshire, Nottinghamshire, Cheshire, South Yorkshire, Lincolnshire, Lancashire, Durham, North Wales, Strathclyde, Grampian, West Midlands, Avon and Somerset, Thames Valley, Essex, Dyfed-Powys, West Mercia, Hampshire, Greater Manchester and Gwent.
- Professor David Bellamy, the RSPCA, the Vegetarian Society and the Tidy Britain Group.

The report and the children's drawings were used in a crime prevention exhibition staged by South Yorkshire Police and by the Elton Community Project. The subject was also adapted for a drama improvisation workshop by the Nexstage Theatre Company.

The campaign received extensive media coverage, including all five national radio stations, coverage on 243 local radio stations, reports in four national daily newspapers and extensive coverage in regional newspapers and specialist publications. Some of the newspaper reports had headings which reinforced the message:

Children becoming caring and sensible. Clean up your act, say children of the nineties. Children register disapproval of drugs, alcoholism and vandalism. Putting the case for kids. Praise for wise words from children 'Ban them for life', that's the way youngsters feel about drink-drivers.

The total 'opportunities to see' figure was 18,246,000 readers. The total budget was £45,000 and the cost of the campaign to the Co-op was £2.46 per 1000 opportunities to see.

CASE DISCUSSION

This case describes just one small part of the CWS comprehensive public relations programme, but is interesting because it is another striking example of the value of presenting major issues for the consideration of young people. As in other examples, the enthusiastic reaction of young boys and girls is almost overwhelming. The results help to counteract current fears about the attitudes and behaviour of youngsters.

The objective of the campaign was somewhat limited, although quite important – to reinforce the use of the slogan 'The Co-op, the people who care'. The results of the essay and drawing competitions showed that the young people of Britain also care very much about their future. The idea of supporting the programme by producing a new board game was an ingenious way of widening the scope of the message.

6

Transport and Energy

Case 6.1 Partnership for improved air travel

BACKGROUND

Since the US airline industry was deregulated in 1978, passenger loads doubled but system capacity — measured in number of airports, runways, air travel control facilities and number of personnel — failed to keep pace. The result was a drastic increase in flight delays, passenger inconvenience and consumer and shipping costs, with the airlines frequently bearing the public's blame.

The aviation industry wanted to shift public focus to aviation system capacity issues and bring pressure to bear on the federal government for remedial action.

RESEARCH

Burson-Marsteller initially conducted 61 interviews with Congressional committee staff, aviation media and associations concerned with air travel issues. The objective was to assess the major problems facing the industry, the real or perceived causes of these problems, and the required remedial action.

There was uniform awareness of the increase in demand on the air transport system and of the strain being felt. Most were familiar with the federal Aviation Trust Fund — supported by an eight per cent federal ticket tax plus fuel and cargo taxes.

Nearly all said that insufficient funds were being spent by the government to remedy the capacity crisis and that a lack of leadership by the Federal Aviation Administration (FAA) and Congress were the main problems.

Airline scheduling and use of hub-and-spoke systems were viewed as aggravating factors. A thorough literature and media search was conducted to support a baseline assessment of public opinion, provide data for development of position papers and other materials, and to build outreach target lists.

PLANNING

Given the public's willingness to apportion some, if not most, of the blame for the aviation capacity crisis to the airlines, it was concluded that the proposed programme must recognise the limits of airline industry credibility. Therefore it was decided that it was essential to have visible sponsorship of the programme outside the airlines.

The initial 140-page plan reviewed the situation, objectives and proposed strategies and outlined a two-year, three-phase grassroots education and mobilisation campaign.

- **Phase one** was 'preparation' which included refinement of the theme, training of spokespersons, coalition organising and audience and message testing.
- **Phase two**, 'kick-off', entailed a satellite news conference originating in Washington DC, and the simultaneous launch of national advertising and direct mail campaigns.
- **Phase three**, 'Education, Persuasion and Mobilisation' included government relations, national coalition building, grassroots mobilisation, a speakers' bureau, publicity, industry communications and continuing research. A flow chart and a two-year budget were also agreed.

The objective was to target decision makers in Washington (both in Congress and the Executive Branch) and surround them with pressure from a broad coalition of forces. This combination included national opinion leaders and representatives of national corporate, professional and labour associations. The entire aviation industry also participated, including employees, suppliers and the travel industry. Other supporters came from public interest, academic and non-profit organisations. Seldom has any coalition embraced such a wide range of supporters.

IMPLEMENTATION

The programme was named the 'Partnership for Improved Air Travel' and a logo was adopted and educational brochures and advertising copy were produced. The programme was launched on 12 April 1988 with:

- 118 media involved in a 12-city satellite teleconference, including 34 local newscasts, 'Good Morning America', the financial news network and CNN;
- direct mail recruitment kits sent to 304,245 frequent flyers in targeted congressional districts;
- recruitment/educational advertisements in major newspapers and magazines.

Written activity reports and planning documents were prepared for both the bi-weekly steering committee meetings and the quarterly board meetings. By March 1990, membership had grown to 250,000 concerned citizens recruited mainly through 14 million brochures inserted in the major airlines frequent flyer mailings; 7800 community leaders in targeted congressional districts, recruited by telephone; and 43 diverse national supporting groups, including the Air Line Pilots Association, the US Conference of Mayors, the National Consumers League, the American Society of Travel Agents and the National Air Traffic Controllers Association. These various groups published articles, distributed Partnership literature to their members and participated in media events. By April 1990, the following had been produced or arranged:

1. Bi-monthly newsletters – one each for media, members and allies.
2. Media tours in 36 major cities – press conferences, editorial board meetings etc.
3. Radio talk shows in 21 targeted cities.
4. Eight major press conferences.
5. 83 different press releases.
6. Aviation facility tours for media in 12 cities, including air traffic control towers, radar rooms etc.
7. Four video news releases via satellite.
8. One 12-city satellite media tour.
9. Spokesperson training for eight individuals.
10. Monthly in-flight magazine columns for use by all the airlines.
11. Testimony before Congress and the US Department of Transportation.
12. 42 Partnership speeches before Rotary clubs, chambers of commerce and other local organisations.
13. Multiple exhibits at government and industry conferences.

Partnership members were mobilised in the summer of 1988 to send thousands of letter to Presidential campaign directors, urging the candidates to give priority attention to air capacity issues. Two thousand two hundred telegrams were sent from constituents to US House Ways and Means Committee members on an airline ticket tax issue; and tens of thousands of letters and airline receipts to the US Senate in support of a Federal Aviation Administration reform bill.

Continuing research was an important feature of the project. The first ever comprehensive study of the impact of civil aviation on the US economy was commissioned. The study quantified the tremendous economic effect of civil aviation on the nation, all 50 states and 10 key metropolitan areas in terms of economic activity, percentages of gross national product and the number of jobs attributed to aviation. The study took into account every aviation sector – commercial and general aviation, civil aircraft manufacturing, suppliers, trade associations, travel agents, retail and air cargo – and all 16,949 civil airports in the United States. The resulting economic impact statement was sent to every member of Congress and key media outlets throughout the nation as further evidence of the importance of expanding aviation capacity to ensure continued economic growth.

Partnership members were surveyed periodically to assess their views on evolving aviation issues and to gauge their response to the efforts of the campaign. The Partnership conducted two public opinion polls – in November 1988 and December 1989 – and the results were given wide media exposure. Both polls showed that the American people favoured expanding the national aviation system as the best way to reduce delays, rather than restricting the number of flights.

The programme envisioned a two-year $15 million budget. The plan and budget were refined each quarter to take full advantage of unfolding events and opportunities, and to respond to new insights gained from the continuing research, surveys of Partnership members, media analyses etc. Special programmes, such as press conferences and mass mailings were budgeted separately. Actual expenditures never deviated more than four per cent from the quarterly budgets.

A steering committee composed of Washington representatives of funding corporations and supporting associations met bi-weekly to monitor the programme. Great care was taken to ensure that all programme elements – the messages, the vehicles and the timing – all worked together, reinforcing each other and reflecting the most current possible information about audience attitudes and the flow of actions and decisions affecting air transportation.

EVALUATION

The Partnership succeeded in focusing the attention of the news media and the public on the severe capacity crisis affecting the US civil aviation system. The campaign had also succeeded in changing the public's perception that the airlines were to blame for the capacity crisis. The programme identified, educated and mobilised America's civil aviation constituency to pressure Congress and the Executive Branch for specific action to remedy the crisis.

Substantial media coverage in all 50 states, a host of editorial endorsements and floods of correspondence from constituents moved Congress to introduce legislation and caused the Secretary of Transportation to declare in February 1990 that aviation system capacity expansion had become one of the Bush Administration's highest priorities.

The Burson-Marsteller team had created a highly motivated grassroots organisation – the broadest aviation coalition in history – to serve the interests of aviation and the welfare of the nation well beyond the life of the project.

One measure of the Partnership's success in re-orienting national policies is seen in a recent federal report. This stated that by 1991 US air traffic delays reached a five-year low as key airports expanded runways and other facilities and new technology for bad weather landings and takeoffs was installed by the federal government.

Much of the credit for the shifting of funds and heightened interest in aviation infrastructure lies with the 'Partnership for Improved Air Travel'.

CASE DISCUSSION

The United States is a huge country, the airlines are an integral part of the country's economy and the population's commercial and personal life, yet it was felt that the Federal Aviation Authority (FAA) and Congress were indifferent to its current needs. This case study shows how a well-researched campaign, implemented on a nation-wide canvas, can achieve a satisfactory change of policy.

The objectives were clear – to achieve increased funding and a better sense of leadership from the FAA which would improve the whole spectrum of air travel in the United States. If the main objective was straightforward, the means of achieving the desired results was far from transparent. The initial research was encapsulated in a 140-page plan which analysed the whole problem in detail and recommended a comprehensive two-year, three-phase plan for a lobbying and educational programme on a nation-wide scale.

Perhaps the most vital decision was to form a partnership of all concerned parties, to avoid the programme being dismissed as simply self-interest on the part of the airlines. In public relations practice, there is often a fine line between the public interest and legitimate self-interests, but if a campaign is carried out openly and fairly, as in this instance, there is no need to worry about criticism.

The choice of a title is always very important. A really appropriate title can help considerably, while an ambiguous or obscure one can be a great handicap. In this instance, the title 'Partnership for Improved Air Travel' was well chosen. It made the main objective of the campaign very clear and emphasised the fact that it was a partnership of all those seeking improved air transport arrangements and facilities.

Case 6.2 Women and energy

BACKGROUND

In 1983, the Kenya Government launched the Special Energy Programme under the Ministry of Energy. Within the programme was the Women in Energy project sponsored by German Technical Cooperation (GTZ), which focused on the improvement of conditions for rural women.

One of the main features of the Women in Energy project was the introduction of an improved wood fuel stove, the *Maendeleo Jiko*. This was considered to be very important for the following reasons:

1. Electricity in Kenya is still far beyond the reach of 74 per cent of the population, electrical appliances even more so.
2. The need for wood energy continued to grow at an alarming rate.
3. Reforestation efforts could not even match current demand.

RESEARCH

Several research projects were undertaken by GTZ to find a suitable jiko which could be distributed *en masse* to the rural population. The jiko had to be simple, cheap, efficient and long-lasting. After three years of experimentation, the Maendeleo Jiko was introduced, but six years later it was recognised that a thoroughly professional communication strategy was needed to market the jiko more effectively.

PLANNING

Yolanda Tavares Public Relations Ltd was appointed with a brief to remedy this communication failure and to propose and produce relevant material to support the entire Women in Energy Maendeleo Jiko project. The programme was to be targeted at users – the rural women, government policymakers and non-governmental organisations in similar fields whose support GTZ needed.

Government field workers were to be utilised to carry the Maendeleo Jiko message to the rural communities with whom they were in constant touch and had previously established a rapport. The donors in Germany were also a vital target group.

One of the major challenges facing the public consultancy was the low literacy rate of the rural women, who differed so fundamentally from their urban sisters. It was essential to emphasise the numerous benefits of the Maendeleo Jiko:

- saving of wood;
- less smoke emission than the traditional three-stone open fire and therefore more hygienic;
- cheap to make;
- safe for children.

These advantages were to be stressed together with encouragement to plant trees and conserve wood fuel.

After a series of meetings and visits to GTZ Nairobi head-quarters, it was agreed to produce various promotional materials — a logo, a users handbook, a calendar, a corporate brochure, a sign for stockists, posters, a video and special kangas.

- **Logo**
  To establish a distinct identity, a new, highly distinctive logo symbolising Women and Energy was produced (see Figure 11).
- **Handbook**
  A simple illustrated Do-it-Yourself handbook, in both English and Kiswahili (the national language), was required urgently. The handbook would illustrate how easily the jiko could be constructed and contain information on its benefits, the availability of jiko liner (the only material to be bought), and maintenance.

  Cognisance was taken of the fact that government reports showed that rural women were progressing in adult literacy classes, and that reading simple English and Swahili would not be a major problem. It was also realised that adult education programmes lacked reading material, a fact which provided an extra dimension to this manual.
- **Calendars**
  It was suggested to GTZ that a colourful calendar should be produced depicting the Women in Energy project. Calendars in Kenya are a very popular communication medium, particularly in rural communities where they are never thrown away but used as wall decorations.

Figure 11 The 'Women and Energy' logo

- **Corporate brochure**
  It was suggested to produce a small brochure for policy makers, giving an overall picture of the Women in Energy project. Here too, the design and editorial would be kept as simple as possible in order to reach a large rural audience.
- **Signs for stockists**
  Special signs would be produced for display by shops selling the ceramic liner, the only material needed to be bought by the women when building the jiko.
- **Posters**
  Posters would be displayed at agricultural shows, field days, at public rallies and for general circulation to create awareness of the campaign.
- **Video production**
  A special video would cover project activities for the benefit of field officers, for training purposes and for sending to the donor country.
- **Kangas**
  A traditional Kenyan sarong which is used widely by women would be designed and produced to motivate field workers and women's groups.

The handbook

The most urgent requirement was for the production of the Do-it-Yourself handbook. This was needed to serve as an instructional aid for the field workers, and also to leave with the women jiko makers after field demonstrations. This project was therefore started first.

Before actual production of the handbook could commence there were a number of preparatory steps necessary. These were:

1. experimenting to find out how to construct the jiko;
2. having a demonstration at GTZ Nairobi headquarters;
3. taking step-by-step photographs of the actual construction;
4. writing a simple explanatory text for approval by the client which was then translated into Kiswahili;
5. briefing the artist to prepare simple drawings using the text and photographs as guidelines.

It was proposed to allow two months for production but this was subject to countless client delays and it took seven months before the brochure was printed. The delays were caused by client consultations with field workers and the various women's groups, notably the umbrella women's movement in Kenya, *KANU Maendeleo ya Wanawake* (development for women). The stove, Maendeleo Jiko, is in fact named after this movement. To save costs, local paper was used and 100,000 copies were printed and dispatched to the field.

The calendar

A bilingual calendar was designed to carry the message of the improved stove throughout the year. This four-page calendar depicted:

1. women planting trees;
2. women constructing the wood stove;
3. a woman cooking in a smokeless hygienic environment, with children playing safely beside her;
4. a woman serving food cooked quickly and easily using the jiko.

The calendar featured very simple artwork which the women could easily identify with. Five thousand calendars were printed, with a reprint of a further 1000. The calendars were distributed to women's groups and all concerned with the programme. The 1991 calendars were produced using two pictures from the 1990 calendar (to save on costs) plus two newly designed pictures, together with a slightly different design. For 1992, 10,000 calendars were ordered using these same pictures but again with a slightly modified design.

The corporate brochure

The corporate brochure was printed and distributed to the various ministries concerned – the Ministry of Energy, the Ministry of

Agriculture and the Ministry of Culture and Social Services. Copies were also sent to non-governmental organisations concerned with tree planting, environmental protection and rural community, extension officers and for use in training seminars. The initial print run was 50,000 and a further 6000 were ordered.

EVALUATION

Since the introduction of Maendeleo Jiko in 1986, 50,000 stoves have been installed in rural homes. The target for 1992 was 180,000 stoves. More than 5000 women's groups have participated in the stove disseminating programme and more groups will be involved in future. More production centres will help to meet the demand because the activities have spread from the five original districts to 14 districts and requests from other districts are being received.

The logo and the Maendeleo Jiko have become synonymous. The magazine of the Intermediate Technology Development Group reported in April 1991 that '... the most serious problem with the Maendeleo stove was satisfying the ever-growing demand'.

Reports from field workers involved in demonstrations emphasised the value of the supporting materials – the handouts, posters, kangas, calendars, handbooks and the brochures.

TAILPIECE

The success of the programme has resulted in the work being continued on an increased level. One hundred thousand A1 full colour posters are being produced, deliberately incorporating the calendar pictures which have become so familiar in rural homes. A video is being produced describing the Women and Energy activities in Nyanza Province for showing at seminars, exhibitions and at donor agencies. A special kanga has been designed bearing the Women in Energy logo and message, to be printed on 35,000 metres of material. The kangas will be used as incentives for staff working on the project.

CASE DISCUSSION

With sponsorship from the German Technical Cooperation Agency, the Kenya Government was able to launch an imaginative plan to improve the living conditions of rural women. After considerable research, a practical answer was found to the need for a simple, cheap, efficient and long-lasting wood-stove. The problem, however, was how to publicise and familiarise the new product among the rural women who would benefit from its adoption.The challenge was a familiar one. A new cooker has been produced, with many special advantages, but how can its availability be brought to the notice of the women who should welcome it and adopt its use? In a typical developed country, usual marketing methods would be employed. This would include advertising on television and in the press and seeking reports and comments in the women's magazines and other media. In Kenya, however, this does not apply. Rural women have a low literacy rate and differ fundamentally from their urban sisters.

The public relations policy was, therefore, to work through women's groups and their field workers who come into direct contact with the rural women. The production of materials to assist them in their demonstration of the new cooker was a priority. The handbook was specially useful and although it was a pity that production was delayed so long, at least all the interested parties were happy with it before it was published.

In general, the case shows how considerable initiative is required to secure results when normal communication methods are not available. It is to be hoped that steps are also being taken to reduce illiteracy and to improve living conditions in the rural areas so that general living standards can more closely approximate to those enjoyed in the urban areas.

New circumstances have arisen in Kenya since the holding of multi-party democratic elections in 1992. This should encourage further aid programmes which would assist the development of beneficial schemes of this kind.

Case 6.3 The story of the 'SeaCat'

BACKGROUND

The introduction of the new Hoverspeed *SeaCat* by Sea Containers Ltd in 1990 provided an opportunity to secure excellent exposure in the international media by attempting to win the Hales Trophy for the Blue Riband of the Atlantic.

The first SeaCat, 'Hoverspeed Great Britain' was built in Tasmania by International Catamarans, and it was decided to use its delivery voyage to Britain to challenge for the Blue Riband. The Blue Riband can be obtained by any craft, but the challenge for the Hales Trophy for the Blue Riband of the Atlantic must be accepted by the Hales Trustees. Under the regulations, the craft must be a passenger carrying vessel and must not refuel during the specified journey from the Ambrose Light to Bishop's Rock. All other contenders for the trophy had been built specifically for the challenge and did not carry passengers. The previous record set by the SS United States in 1952 was made by an ocean-going liner.

PLANNING

An official challenge was accepted by the Hales Trustees in May 1989 but the planning of the public relations programme did not begin until the craft was launched in January 1990.

Sea Containers Ltd commissioned a series of five video news releases (VNRs) to provide suitable footage for television stations in Europe, the United States and Australia. These VNRs were used widely in the USA. The first VNR was shot in Tasmania and covered the initial sea trials of the SeaCat. The second VNR covered its arrival in New York and the third showed the start of the challenge attempt at the Ambrose Light off the US East Coast. The fourth VNR included coverage of the SeaCat completing its successful attempt at Bishop's Rock, off the Scilly Isles in the UK. The fifth filmed the SeaCat's arrival at Falmouth. The footage was shot by a video camera-man aboard the craft for the duration of the challenge. Radio links were used to produce short feature pieces in the form of interviews with the crew, and these were released to television stations throughout the UK.

In addition to providing radio and video tapes to the media, a 24-hour control room was set up at Sea Containers head office in London. This had six direct lines and a separate fax number and other administrative support was provided. There were direct telephone links with the ship and it was possible for journalists to interview members of the crew. Photographs of the departure from the USA and the actual crossing were flown back and distributed throughout the European, US and Australian press.

The in-house public relations department in London was complemented by three public relations consultancies appointed to handle media relations in Australia, US and France.

IMPLEMENTATION

Brochures and promotional material were produced for use as background material and press packs. These included:

- a brochure describing the challenge attempt;
- a profile of the Hoverspeed Great Britain crew;
- technical information about the craft;
- a route map; and
- a series of colour and black and white photographs.

Clothing for the crew was provided by sponsorship from Timberland and Omega provided watches and digital clocks situated on board the craft and in the control room to time the journey.

The entire event was stage managed by the in-house department of 14 people, with ground support from Hoverspeed personnel in Dover and Portsmouth. There was constant liaison with the Hales Trustees. This began with a press conference in May 1989 when the challenge was made and accepted by the Trustees. Further press conferences were held before the start of the journey on 19 June 1991.

A set of emergency procedures was also established but fortunately these did not have to be used.

Schedule of events

1. 7 May–19 June 1990. Arrival of craft in New York

The craft left Tasmania on 7 May 1990 and a press briefing was held in London on 21 May, when the president of the company,

James B Sherwood, outlined the details of the transatlantic challenge to the national media. The first VNR was issued at this press briefing.

A second press conference was held in New York for US media as soon as the craft arrived. Photographs of the craft in New York were issued internationally to create interest during the run-up to the challenge.

2. 19 June–21 June. Period of challenge

As soon as the craft crossed the starting line at the Ambrose Light, near New York, the control of the event passed to the control room at Sea Containers House in London. The London control room was manned 24 hours a day. This gave the UK, US, continental and Australian media direct access to the latest information.

Interviews were arranged for radio and TV stations with the captain of the craft via Satcom connected conference calls routed through the control room. Photographs of the captain were also made available to illustrate the broadcast.

3. 23 June. Hoverspeed Great Britain arrives in the UK

Media facilities were organised at the Scilly Islands for all the major Sunday national newspapers to take aerial photographs of the craft at Bishop's Rock as it completed the challenge.

Video news release no 3 was shot at the same time to cover the successful conclusion of the transatlantic challenge. This footage was processed in Southampton and fed to all the major TV stations in time for the lunchtime news programmes.

From Bishop's Rock the craft made its way to Falmouth, where a news conference was staged for local media. Celebration photographs were wired immediately via Press Association and Associated Press.

A limited number of local Portsmouth media were invited to join the craft at Falmouth for the final part of the journey to its home port at Portsmouth. During the four-hour journey, the local Portsmouth papers and radio journalists were able to telephone stories announcing the craft's arrival in Portsmouth later that evening. This ensured a turn-out of over 10,000 people to welcome the vessel upon its arrival at 8 pm that evening.

As soon as the craft docked, the captain, John Lloyd and the builder, Bob Clifford were greeted by Hoverspeed hostesses and a press conference and photo calls were arranged for the media.

All publicity material and press information was generated by the London office and forwarded to subsidiary offices elsewhere in Europe, the US and Australia for distribution.

EVALUATION

In the period immediately before the challenge and after its successful conclusion, over 24 news releases were issued throughout Europe, the US and Australia, and more than 520 calls were logged. As a result of the issue of the video news releases, over two hours of prime time television was achieved in the UK alone. It was considered that the budget of £750,000 was more than covered by the estimated £3 million of publicity generated by the event.

Following the publicity generated during the Blue Riband challenge, Hoverspeed's reservations department was inundated with inquiries from travel agents and the general public requesting information and reservations. A survey conducted a little later showed that 80 per cent of people interviewed recognised the name of SeaCat. The wide publicity generated by the event also helped to ensure international recognition of the new craft.

Since Hoverspeed Great Britain's arrival in Britain in June 1990, a further four SeaCats have been brought to Europe, this time via the Indian Ocean. Hoverspeed currently operates three services on the English Channel, a service from Scotland to Northern Ireland, and a fifth craft has been chartered to run between mainland Italy and the island of Sardinia under the name 'Sardinia Express'.

CASE DISCUSSION

If a new product or service is to be introduced, there is a choice between using public relations, or advertising, or a combination of the two. If creative thinking (or some fortuitous circumstances) can be used to arouse wide public interest, the public relations choice is likely to be the most effective and will certainly be much cheaper. The decision by Sea Containers to challenge for the Blue Riband was very courageous for, while a successful attempt would generate wide and favourable publicity, a failure would be counterproductive.

Having issued the challenge, and having it accepted by the Hales Trustees, the record breaking attempt fitted Hoverspeed's image of offering fast crossing and revolutionary technology. The company made sure that all the arrangements were completed in good time and ample resources were provided for a thoroughly professional approach which secured a very satisfactory outcome of the whole project.

After the successful completion of the challenge for the Hales

Trophy of the Atlantic, souvenir items were produced for on-board sale. In addition to this, there were a number of events to promote the SeaCat. When the trophy was officially handed over by the Hales Trustees, Hoverspeed Great Britain was sailed from her home port to berth close to Tower Bridge for an official reception on board. Lord Callaghan presented the Hales Trophy, on behalf of the Trustees, to James B Sherwood, the founder and president of the parent company, Sea Containers. During the time that the vessel was berthed on the Thames at Tower Bridge, the opportunity was taken to stage a number of special events. One of these was a travel trade reception so that travel agents from all over London could see this exciting new craft.

The video news releases which were produced to cover the challenge are still used to provide footage to television companies for travel features and to production companies for corporate videos and television commercials. For example, Racal recently used footage of the SeaCat in their corporate video and the Boulogne Chamber of Commerce recently produced a commercial which featured the SeaCat. Not only are these excerpts used by external companies, but also internally by the Sea Containers Group in their own corporate video and for induction training for new staff.

The Hales Trophy is still with Hoverspeed and creates further publicity. It has been on display in the Science Museum in London, the Maritime Museum in Liverpool and at the Victoria and Albert Museum where it was part of a display of sporting trophies. Hoverspeed, as the current holder of the trophy, is consistently mentioned in any new attempts across the Atlantic.

This case study illustrates a classic example of how an initiative with potentially great prestige and publicity value can be promoted successfully if adequate resources and budget are provided to make it possible for the public relations team to exploit the possibilities to the full.

Case 6.4 Establishing the Vattenfall Group as the leading energy supplier in Sweden

BACKGROUND

Vattenfall is the largest power group in Scandinavia and the fifth largest in Europe. It started operations 85 years ago. Today, it supplies half of Sweden's electric power. It generates 50 per cent from hydro power and 50 per cent from nuclear power. Vattenfall is active in electric power production and sales, in heat, energy services and natural gas. Its market is gradually expanding outside Sweden. Its main customers are energy companies, industrial corporations and railway operators. Power is supplied to some 700,000 retail customers.

The Vattenfall Group consists of the parent company, Vattenfall AB, and more than 80 subsidiaries. Revenues exceed US$3.2 billion, with 9300 employees.

Electricity is part of everyone's daily life, at home, work and at play. In energy-rich Sweden, it is taken for granted, something one rarely thinks about.

When Vattenfall was reorganised from being a state-owned public utility to a limited liability company in 1992, and had to face more open competition internationally, the company's corporate culture was modernised. As a public utility, Vattenfall had maintained a rather low profile. Consequently, the company was known to a far lesser degree than its importance to the country justified. Deregulation – and a possible privatisation in the future – created the need for an active programme to raise its profile.

The group's overall public relations strategy

Vattenfall's group management regards systematic and sustained public relations activities as one of the most important ways of implementing the company's strategies and achieving the established objectives. Public relations is an integral part of management responsibility within Vattenfall. The Vattenfall public relations model has set the standard for the whole of the Swedish power industry.

RESEARCH

Vattenfall's public relations departments, centrally and in the business areas, continually conduct comprehensive surveys and analysis activities. This provides the base for the group's total public relations activities. Image surveys with the general public are conducted each year. In addition, prioritised target groups, such as customers, politicians, the financial community, teachers and journalists, are surveyed several times annually.

Moreover, public knowledge and opinion concerning nuclear energy and hydro power is surveyed twice a year. Vattenfall's public relations department also continuously monitors the image surveys conducted externally in which Vattenfall is compared with other companies in Sweden.

While all these surveys cover the corporate image field, similar surveys among customers are carried out by the marketing units. The combined results are carefully analysed by the public relations staff and discussed at top management meetings. They provide a reliable basis for establishing the annual information strategy. Based on this strategy and analysis, various information goals and related activities are determined.

PLANNING

The general public in Sweden is very well aware of Vattenfall, its size in very broad terms and its responsibility for hydro power production and distribution. However, very little is known about its real size in terms of market share, technological competence, and visions for the future of Swedish energy supply, both domestic and international. This great paradox, with which Vattenfall's public relations staff is struggling, is due to the public's favourable access to energy at low cost. The public take this relationship for granted. This is an unfair consequence of the company's efficiency.

The research indicated the target objectives of the 1993 high profile programme which would cover the whole country and involve both print and broadcast media.

Objectives

The programme would be aimed at the following:

1. strengthening knowledge about Vattenfall's significance for Swedish living standards and industrial growth;

2. providing overall support for marketing activities;
3. clarifying the company's corporate visions and concepts to external key publics and the general public;
4. spreading the same message to its own staff via advertisements in the daily press to inspire pride in the company among employees.

Identification of publics

The target publics were identified as opinion leaders, customers, financial markets, politicians and the media.

The content of the message

The programme was aimed at repositioning Vattenfall and changing the company's image:

From	To
unknown	well known
minor importance	important in many ways
cold and abstract	warm and reliable
heavy and slow	flexible and efficient
production oriented	customer oriented
passive monopoly	active, open market entrepreneur
electricity generation	energy services
exploiting nature	nature conservation, environmentally sound

The goal of the campaign

As a result of the campaign, it was hoped that opinion formers and the public would gain a clear perception of Vattenfall as a company which is:

● efficient and customer oriented;
● environmentally aware;
● balanced in its view on the environment;
● long-term focused;
● sympathetic with personal financial goals.

So far as the printed media was concerned the goal was to have 40 per cent of the 15–75 age group exposed to at least one of the advertisements and that more than 10 per cent would have a more positive view of Vattenfall after the campaign.

For television, only exposure figures can be measured and

therefore the goal was set at 60 per cent of those in the 24–60 age group which has access to commercial television.

Media selection for advertising

The media selection resulted in advertisements in a broad range of newspapers, magazines and television, including national dailies, regional dailies, local dailies and business magazines.

The media selection was carefully analysed through computer-based media research. Five full-page advertisements were specially prepared, and a 35-second film related to the advertisements was produced for showing on commercial television.

The public relations message

Internally, the campaign was announced in advance through a personal message from the group chief executive officer sent directly to 350 members of senior management and through a folder to each employee, aimed at preparing the whole organisation for follow-up activities.

To create interest in Vattenfall and its role in Swedish society as well as the importance of energy supply in everyday life, it was decided to focus on a number of real-life cases, examples which would gain the attention of the reader-audience. Each case was linked to psychological archetypes – life, jobs, the future, freedom and joy. The examples were dramatised in text and photographs.

The total budget for the campaign was US$900,000. The whole programme – from concept, through to goal-setting, implementation, evaluation and follow-up – was reviewed and discussed in several stages by group management, and the group's board of directors was kept informed about the campaign's purpose and content in relation to long-term goals as well as short-term objectives.

IMPLEMENTATION

Advertisements

Five special full-page advertisements were used (see Figure 12 for one example).

1. **Life**
   Little Malin, a newborn baby with a severe heart problem,

HERE IN SWEDEN FREEDOM OF SPEECH DOES NOT HANG BY A SLENDER THREAD.

Power costs eat up between three and five per cent of the total costs of producing a major daily. This takes in manufacturing the paper, running the editorial machine and printing the newspaper.

Quite a sizeable bite in other words. But without electricity the flow of news would dry up completely.

The media are a cornerstone of our democracy. So long as they function smoothly. But "the fourth estate" could all-too-easily be silenced if the supply of energy to TV stations and printing presses were cut off. And then freedom of speech would hang on a very slender thread indeed.

Happily, Sweden has a reliable energy supply with few power cuts. Vattenfall deliver energy to a large part of the Swedish daily press, to many TV and radio stations, and to the major paper mills.

Paper is one of the most energy-intensive components in a newspaper. Without paper there would be no newspapers. Without electricity there would be no paper. In the paper industry, production is round-the-clock and downtimes enormously costly.

So the reliable and effective supply of energy is critical to keeping costs—and consequently the price of paper—down. This means we can produce an abundance of newspapers, so that many voices can be heard.

The media constitute an invaluable force in our society. Electricity enables us to hear what they have to say.

VATTENFALL
EMPOWERING SWEDEN

Figure 12 One of the full-page advertisements used in the Vattenfall, Sweden, campaign

required advanced surgery at the Karolinska University Hospital of Stockholm, where Vattenfall not only supplies the energy, but is also responsible for all the security and backup systems. Without a reliable energy supply, Malin would not have had her 'second chance'.

2. **Jobs**
   The crystal industry. Through cost efficiency and investment on the one hand, and passion for quality and much stamina on the other, this old industry has survived despite many difficulties. Glass works today are fuelled with electricity, which means lower costs and also less impact on the environment. Perseverance, creativity and electricity have saved the industry.

3. **The future**
   Junior ice hockey team. We all have a dream of the future. In the small town of Lysekil, the local government has been able to keep the 'professional' dreams of young boys alive and also save money – and at the same time the environment – through installing Vattenfall's systems combining heating, cooling and lighting in the municipal ice hall.

4. **Freedom**
   At the printers. Cheap, safe electricity is crucial for producing paper and print, and without electricity there would be no broadcasting. Sweden has a very rich media and thus freedom of speech – and eventually democracy – is secured.

5. **Joy**
   The rock concert. Being a leading specialist in energy conservation, advising industries and households on how to minimise their energy consumption, Vattenfall also delivers electricity to some of the largest concert halls in Sweden, where a lot of energy is consumed. With effective everyday saving, waste can be afforded on special occasions.

A film for television

A film was produced, illustrating electricity's omnipresence – in heavy industries, creative areas and households. The film ends with a hungry little boy opening the fridge late at night.

The TV spot was screened while the advertisements were being run in the press. The message was that Vattenfall is important for Sweden, for business and for the man in the street and that – through its reliable supply of economical and environmentally sound electricity – Vattenfall is a major driving force in Sweden.

Pilot study

During a trial period, the TV film was shown during the spring, and was evaluated quantitatively and qualitatively and revised prior to the start of the campaign. The message had been perceived properly and favourably, but the sign-off could be better understood if made more distinct. Accordingly, a five-second revision, plus a strengthened logotype and closing line, were added to the final version.

Since TV advertising was not used by Vattenfall's competitors, the series was extended on TV in the autumn campaign. The print campaign ran in morning dailies all over Sweden from 8–23 October, and in the business press in November. The TV spot was broadcast from 4–20 October.

EVALUATION

Awareness

Vattenfall systematically and continuously measure the awareness and perception of its profile campaigns. Interviews with 1000 randomly selected persons yielded the following results concerning the effect of the advertising in the press media.

- Immediately after the campaign, 44 per cent stated that they had seen the advertisements.
- The advert with the baby had the highest recognition figure.
- The intention of capturing the attention of various age groups worked out as planned. For example, the rock concert advert was viewed by a greater number of teenagers.
- The adverts supplemented one another and increased the total viewing level.
- Interest in reading the copy in the adverts yielded a 54 per cent 'yes' response, which is high for this type of measurement. The TV campaign also had a high viewer figure.
- Of the 4,552,000 persons in the target group (20–64 age group), 62 per cent of the target group, or slightly more than 2.8 million people, saw the TV spot at least once, 40 per cent saw it twice, 25 per cent saw it three times, and 14 per cent saw it four times.

Continued profiling

Combined with other profiling efforts during 1993, this campaign improved Vattenfall's image in line with the established strategy. The profiling into a 'modern, customer-oriented energy company' could be seen distinctly in the image surveys. The tendency was clearly positive — the rate of change corresponded with the projected level. Accordingly, during 1994 and in future years, Vattenfall continued and will continue to work systematically with new campaigns, among other activities, to create a distinct view of Vattenfall as the modern energy company it already is and will achieve in due course its place in the top ranks of European energy companies.

CASE DISCUSSION

This is an interesting example of a major industrial group which obviously believes in the importance of public acceptance of its vital role in the national economy. Moreover, it is prepared to allocate a very substantial annual budget to public relations.

Top management and the public relations staff jointly plan the ideal parameters of the planned campaign and monitor its progress.

Research is used extensively in analysing and assessing the problems and opportunities confronting the organisation and in deciding the objectives and the methods to be used to achieve them.

The main attempt to secure public attention was through the series of imaginative advertisements. This is a good example of the effective use of advertising in a public relations programme.

The results of the 1993 programme were successful enough for the group to plan similar ambitious public relations programmes in the following years.

7

Health Care and Medicine

Case 7.1 Prostate cancer awareness week

BACKGROUND

Prostate cancer is the second leading cancer killer of American men: about 32,000 American men died of this condition in recent years. Yet despite these frightening statistics, the condition has received scant attention from the American public, physicians and the media.

To ameliorate this situation and to create a favourable environment in which to market its prostate cancer drug, *Eulexin*, Schering decided to sponsor a national prostate cancer awareness week (PCAW). Burson-Marsteller, of New York, worked with Schering to plan this national campaign which was designed to provide a national grassroots screening programme involving a network of hospitals across the United States.

In the previous year, 1989, the results of a pilot programme exceeded expectations by over 50 per cent: 14,600 men received free examinations in 30 states. Having thus confirmed the viability of such a scheme, the target set for 1990 was to make Prostate Cancer Awareness Week truly national and accessible to all men and to all practising urologists.

RESEARCH

An extensive research programme was drawn up to support the 1990 Prostate Cancer Awareness Week. The research programme took into account the experience of the 1989 event. In 1989 several primary and secondary research tools were used to determine awareness and attitudes towards prostate cancer among urologists, men and the media. Telephone interviews with physicians revealed that because of the sensitive nature of the examination, both the physician and patient avoided dealing with the subject.

A national survey of 1017 men of age 18 + showed that:

1. nearly two-thirds of the men surveyed had not had a physical examination within the last year;
2. fewer than half of those who had ever had a physical examination said that a prostate examination was included;
3. only eight per cent of the men interviewed said they had ever discussed prostate cancer with their physicians, despite the fact that it is the most common tumour in men.

Telephone audits of consumer media editors revealed that the subject was difficult to cover in their journals and therefore they shied away from it. To stand a chance of being used, future stories would need to focus on education or information showing that men can survive the disease. Interviews by telephone with staff at key cancer organisations showed that men rarely request information. It was emphasised that prostate cancer needed the same type of celebrity attention as breast cancer has received.

Informal focus groups of Burson-Marsteller staff over the age of 50 revealed men's belief that the examination is painful and the consequences of the disease unpleasant. Secondary research included a widespread media coverage which revealed that prostate cancer stories were very rare.

The need for another awareness week was supported by the undoubted success of the 1989 Prostate Cancer Awareness Week which had achieved a strong positive response to the screening programme from urologists, men aged 40 or over and the media. What began as a pilot programme, with 20 sites and a goal of 5000 men ended with 81 sites and 14,600 men screened.

During the 1989 screening programme, patients completed a standardised questionnaire that gathered information on medical history and demographics. The result of the digital rectal examination was also included on the questionnaire. These forms were analysed during 1990 and when the results were projected against the male population aged 40 or over it was estimated that 1.2 million men may potentially have prostate cancer and that it was grossly undiagnosed due to non-examination.

This data was also being prepared as a peer-review in a medical journal to reinforce the information in the urology community.

PLANNING

The proposed Prostate Cancer Awareness Week had three primary audiences:

- urologists
- men aged 40 or over
- the Schering sales force.

To consider the needs of each of these audiences, a meeting was held in 1990 to plan the September screening.

At the March planning meeting, the decision was made to develop multiple communication channels to encourage all urologists to participate in the programme. Increasing the number of urologists would increase the number of screening examinations that could be offered as well as raising Schering's visibility.

Organisational and logistical issues, including criteria for participation, screening protocol and documentation, coordination of sites and publicity were discussed with the Prostate Cancer Education Council (PCEC). The PCEC is an advisory panel of physicians, health educators and patient support groups that offer guidance on patient issues. The most important issue discussed during this meeting was whether or not a new screening test should be offered. The new test, prostate specific antigen blood test, has promised to be a more accurate and less invasive test than the most common screening procedure, the digital rectal examination. The problem with offering the blood test, however, is its high cost. Nevertheless a majority of the urologists wanted to offer the new blood test and there was a consensus that the public would demand it, so to meet the needs of the target audiences, arrangements were made with manufacturers to donate tests.

Programme strategies were to form alliances with important physician and patient groups; also to ensure access to a national network of hospitals and to provide urologists with practice building tools under Schering's name.

The budget to cover the coordination of local screenings, development of publicity materials and allied costs was $912,000.

EXECUTION

In order to meet the programme objectives of broadening the reach of the programme and generating maximum screening attendance, a four-phase programme was implemented to recruit screening sites, then organise, promote and publicise the screenings.

Recruitment

There was close cooperation with the American Urological

Association (AUA) to recruit their members to participate. A letter from the association's president encouraged all members to participate in this public education campaign. Regular columns in the association's newsletter kept the membership informed about the progress of the programme.

To supplement these efforts and to develop personal relationships, Schering developed an exhibit booth for the AUA's annual meeting. The exhibit booth highlighted all aspects of the programme and allowed the account team to personally communicate the benefits of participation.

Urologists visited the booth to greet national spokesperson Rocky Bleier, a former Pittsburgh football star, whose grandfathers died of prostate cancer. A brochure describing the programme was also distributed. The brochure included a reply postcard to facilitate action.

Prostate Cancer Awareness Week was also pitched to the media attending the conference as well as the local media. The goal was to reinforce the importance of screenings and to encourage urologists attending the conference to sign up.

Organisation

As sites were signed up to provide screening facilities, they were placed in two categories: Tier I and Tier II sited. Tier I sites, representing 20 major cities, were provided with a step-by-step guide helping them to organise their screening arrangements. Materials provided to the sites included posters, advertising copy and patient education brochures. Sites were also provided with a patient questionnaire/exam results to be used to register all patients. The data from these forms would be analysed for new insights into prostate cancer and the results of the research would be publicised in the consumer and medical media. Burson-Marsteller was also available for counsel on logistics, promotional tactics and publicity strategy.

Tier II sites were provided with the same support material and guidance. However, the national scope of the programme made it impossible to coordinate the media effort for all 750 sites, so Tier II sites were provided with a publicity handbook and press materials that could be tailored for their local media.

In addition to the support of the AUA, other influential third party organisations supported the programme. The Association of Community Cancer Centers recruited member hospitals, and the National Cancer Institute and the National Cancer Care Foundation distributed the consumer brochure.

Promotion

The American Association of Retired Persons, reticent to work with industry, generated grassroots interest in prostate cancer, using a Speaker's Kit that was specifically developed for their health promotion staff.

An advertorial featuring spokesperson Rocky Bleier began to condition the target audience about the importance of prostate cancer awareness. Meanwhile, Schering was promoting its commitment to the urology community through an advertisement in the AUA's membership guide.

Posters and advertising copy were provided for all Tier I and Tier II sites to promote the screenings.

Publicity

An extensive publicity campaign was developed and executed to support the public education campaign. Burson-Marsteller coordinated the writing, distribution and follow-up for the 20 Tier I cities. Reaching the media in these markets with key messages was critical to generating screening attendance.

The campaign was launched with the distribution of public service announcement scripts to radio and television stations nation-wide. Calendar listings were sent to newspapers and magazines. To ensure a fresh angle for the media, the message communicated via the press kit was that the analysis of 1989 data revealed that 1.2 million American men may have prostate cancer, yet most cases go unnoticed because men are not being examined. These press kits were distributed to national and local media. Press material with targeted messages was also sent to black and Hispanic media, encouraging men to attend the screenings.

A 1–800 telephone number was set up so that the media could offer their audiences easy access to information, and material was developed to assist television stations with stories.

EVALUATION

All the different organisations involved in the programme rated it an outstanding success. This subjective evaluation was amply confirmed by the statistics:

- 750 sites nation-wide offered free examinations, more than three times the planned target of 200.

- Urologists have hailed the programme as a great public service and education programme. The president of the American Urological Association sent a letter to the president of Schering commending the company for sponsoring the programme.
- More than 150,000 men availed themselves of the free examinations, six times more than the target figure.
- Media coverage was exceptional:
  — 750 stories appeared in newspapers, reaching a readership in excess of 30 million with the message advising screening;
  — 194 television stories about prostate cancer reached an estimated audience of 23 million;
  — dozens of stories on radio reinforced the message;
  — many stories and news items appeared in the minority media;
  — the media coverage included the *Chicago Tribune*, the *Washington Post, Boston Globe* and dailies in Atlanta, Detroit, Denver, San Diego, Cleveland and Tampa.
- More than 40,000 people called the 1-800-4-CANCER telephone number requesting information on screening sites.

Medical assessment

The Prostate Cancer Education Council issued an interim report to all the organisations which had supported the programme. It stated: 'Early returns and comments from screening sites and other participants show that the week was an unqualified success on all fronts'.

From a medical standpoint, the results can be evaluated by the ratio of the number of men screened to the number referred for further examination. The early returns showed that this ratio varied considerably from one site to another. Twenty per cent was quite common but one or two sites reported 40 per cent referrals.

CASE DISCUSSION

This case, and the following one which deals with breast cancer, raise a question as to the ethics of a manufacturer or organisation sponsoring a national or regional health programme from which it will derive considerable commercial benefit. A distinction should be drawn here between, for example, a manufacturer who mounts a campaign to promote a particular type of food or an over-the-counter medicine with little or no identification of the source of the publicity and this case where Schering's name was closely associated with the project throughout. In many countries, as in Britain, one would expect such a campaign to be initiated and carried out by the National Health Service. The situation is different in the US, as in this case, where the Medicare programme would not be involved.

The success of the pilot scheme in the previous year meant that there was a firm base on which to build. The main problem was to achieve a wide measure of support from the hospitals and the medical specialists, the urologists, to ensure that the demand for screening which would be produced by the publicity of the awareness week could be met adequately.

Perhaps partly as a result of AIDS information programmes there is now less sensitivity about openly discussing medical and sexual matters than hitherto, but a discussion of the prostate gland is not the obvious subject of polite conversation. Natural reticence had to be overcome by plain speaking and strong emphasis on the fact that early diagnosis means saving lives.

The statistics given in the evaluation of the case are a sign of its undoubted success and both Schering and Burson-Marsteller should be well pleased with the results of their efforts. Schering received many accolades from the medical profession, praising their intiative, and the *Eulexin* product manager was given an award during the plenary session of the American Urological Association's annual meeting.

On the broader issue of a pharmaceutical company sponsoring such a national screening project, it is obviously simpler when there is only one prescription drug of its kind on the market. It would be a different and more complex situation if there were approved drugs competing for treatment of the same condition.

Case 7.2 Using Rembrandt to promote health in Australia

BACKGROUND

There is general acceptance that screening has an important part to play in the prevention or early detection of many very serious conditions which threaten life. One of the success stories in this field is the routine screening for breast cancer.

When the Medical Benefit Fund, Australia (MBF) acquired the Sydney Square Breast Clinic they wanted to publicise the new ownership and to increase awareness of the MBF's management policies, especially in the prevention field. Also to reinforce the concept to MBF members of value for money. The breast screening programme was to be targeted mainly at women over 40, and members received a substantial discount over non-members ($A20 compared with $A60).

The philosophy of the MBF management is to encourage partnership with key creative agencies and this case is a good example of public relations and advertising working closely together to form a total communication package.

RESEARCH

The public relations consultants Kathie Melocco & Associates Pty Limited of Sydney carried out research prior to the initiation of the breast cancer campaign, its main objective being to find themes and facts which could be used effectively in providing an understanding of the common problems facing all health funds, including falling membership.

The relevance of private health insurance was being questioned in Australia and concern was being raised regarding its cost. Many people could not see its need or value for money.

PLANNING

The remit to Kathie Melocco & Associates was to develop a public relations strategy that would complement the new advertising campaign which was to feature the famous Rembrandt painting of Bathsheba. The well-known biblical story is illustrated in this picture which shows Bathsheba holding the letter from King David asking her to meet him in secret, a meeting which was to have such tragic consequences. It was painted by Rembrandt in 1654, with his common law wife, Hendrickje Stoffels as the model. In the painting of the left breast of the model there is very clear indication of the distinctive dimpling which is now recognised as an early sign of breast cancer. To an art lover this is a classic Rembrandt painting, but to a doctor this is a classic example of an early tumour.

This dramatic diagnosis which functioned as the basic element of the campaign, was suggested by Dr Joan Croll, Head of the MBF Breast Cancer Clinic. It was used to great effect in the public relations and advertising campaign to encourage women in Sydney to seek screening for early detection of breast cancer at the MBF Sydney Clinic. The advertisements included reproductions of the painting and close-ups of the left breast, and these pictures emphasised the message more clearly than hundreds of words. The story captured the imagination of the print and broadcasting media and the coverage was nationwide. It did not happen by chance, but resulted from the carefully planned and well-orchestrated launch of the campaign which was held at the Intercontinental Hotel in Sydney. Leading women from all walks of life, and representatives of all the various women's interest associations, were invited to lunch and to hear a dramatic presentation of the breast cancer problem (which is a major cause of death among women in Australia) and to hear how routine screening of women over 40 can greatly reduce this threat to life.

The documentation which was prepared and handed out at the launch was most comprehensive. It included notes on the history of the condition which was first recognised in the seventeenth century, with Anne of Austria reputed to have been the first woman to suffer surgery – *without* anaesthetics! The life expectancy of women at that time was only 35 so breast cancer, which predominates in older women, was not such a menace in those far-off days.

The press kit and the slides at the luncheon presentation showed how mammography is carried out painlessly at the clinic and also emphasised the useful role of women in carrying out self-examination checking as a regular routine.

The launch of the programme ran into very few problem areas — somewhat surprising in view of the magnitude and the sensitivity of the subject. There were no new diagnostic or treatment developments in the field of breast cancer to report so there were no natural news angles. However, the launch was received enthusiastically by the media, due largely to lateral angles being developed and issued to the media. Much of the credit is due to Dr Joan Croll, who proved such an excellent spokeswoman and leader of the whole programme.

Media strategy for the launch included pre-placing stories, as well as publicity angles incorporating the value of membership and educational aspects. News releases were sent out systematically to specifically targeted media, as were telephone calls and private meetings. The result was overwhelming media interest and stories continued to be published throughout the duration of the programme.

The response from various sections of the community was very supportive. Female representatives from the police, the Army, the Church, business and commerce, fashion, the theatre, nurses, politicians, lawyers and opinions leaders all attended the launch. These women accepted the role of ambassadors to the female community at large.

Some of the newspaper headlines are worth quoting:

'Help keep Australian women alive'
'Campaign aims for breast cancer alert'
'Message in a masterpiece'
'Campaign to keep women alive'
'Keeping Australian women alive with mammography'

EVALUATION

The campaign was very successful and enquiries at the clinic increased by 700 per cent. A similar campaign was later introduced in other Australian east coast cities. Some statistics emphasise the success of the programme:

- Within the first two weeks of the campaign, the clinic's special information line received 2500 calls. Calls to the clinic for appointments increased from an average of 13 calls a day to an average of 91 calls a day.
- Family planning clinics requested copies of the MBF poster to display in their premises.
- St Vincent's Oncology Unit received hundreds of calls about

breast cancer and asked for copies of the Breast Clinic leaflet for them to give out and copies of the poster to display.

- The New South Wales Health Minister, Peter Collins, personally paid a compliment to the campaign.

CASE DISCUSSION

The MBF Breast Health campaign was undoubtedly a great success, due to its being professionally researched, planned and executed with the clinic staff, the advertising agency and the public relations consultancy working together harmoniously and achieving a high degree of creativity, motivation and dedication.

Using the Rembrandt painting as the central feature may be criticised by some as a 'gimmick' and conventional wisdom warns against the use of gimmicks in public relations, suggesting that they should be confined to publicity use. In fact, gimmicks are quite valid for public relations use, provided the gimmick has a positive relationship to the subject of the programme and is not merely an irrelevancy added on to gain publicity.

It is difficult to think of a gimmick that could be such an integral part of a problem such as the one which the Sydney Square Clinic set out to bring to the notice of the women of Australia. It is true that the clinic wished to increase its membership and to attract women to attend for screening, but the proven benefit of early detection of breast cancer more than justifies the scale of the promotion.

This case study won a trophy in the 1991 IPRA Golden World Awards for Excellence and was also awarded a certificate from the United Nations. By general acclaim, these twin honours were well deserved.

Case 7.3 Aids intervention project in Kenya and Tanzania

BACKGROUND

While the spread of AIDS has become a world-wide problem, its impact has been most serious in Africa. Public relations cannot cure plagues of this kind but it can do valuable work in helping to publicise the problem and educating the public about ways of avoiding contagion. In the 1990 IPRA Golden World Awards for Excellence, a major award was won by an AIDS education programme in Uganda called 'Give a face to AIDS'. This case study also received a special award from the United Nations.

In the 1991 IPRA Golden World Awards, another entry concerning AIDS prevention in Africa won a golden trophy for this case study which describes the imaginative public relations project which was aimed at the education of long-distance truck drivers in Kenya and Tanzania, who were considered to be a particularly vulnerable group.

Thirty-four years ago, a young Nairobi-based surgeon, Sir Michael Wood, saw the need for surgical help in remote rural hospitals. He offered his services and initially travelled by road to these areas. It soon became apparent that travelling by air would allow him to go further afield and so he learnt to fly. Connecting these rural hospitals by radio provided better communication and hence more efficient planning and extension of the service. This surgical service by air and its radio network were the beginning of the East African Flying Doctor Service which started in a temporary building at Wilson Airport, Nairobi. An expanded version of this flying service became the African Medical and Research Foundation (AMREF).

AMREF's mission is simple but fundamental: to improve the health of the people in East Africa, especially those in the rural areas least served by health services. AMREF's overall goal is to identify health needs and to develop, implement and evaluate methods and programmes to meet these needs through service, training and research. AMREF runs a wide variety of innovative projects with an emphasis on appropriate low-cost health care for people in rural areas. Project funds come from government and non-government aid agencies in Africa, Europe and North America as well as from private donors. The Foundation has official relations with WHO, UNICEF and UNDP.

With the onslaught of the scourge of HIV (Human Immuno-deficiency Virus) and AIDS (Acquired Immune-Deficiency Syndrome), epidemiological evidence gathered in East Africa suggested a pattern of sexual transmission of HIV where a few individuals with a high number of sexual partners, such as long-distance truck drivers and barmaids, ran a high risk of acquiring and transmitting the virus which ultimately leads to AIDS.

AMREF considered that attitude and behaviour changes towards sex must be one of the most important approaches for an intervention programme to prevent this problem getting even worse.

RESEARCH

AMREF conducted research on the knowledge, attitudes and practices (KAP) regarding AIDS and sexually transmitted diseases (STD) among long-distance truck drivers, their assistants and their sexual partners on major highways in Kenya and Tanzania. This research was aimed at securing baseline information for rational planning of an intervention programme.

The research findings indicated that the target population had an average of three different sex partners in two months. In a few extreme cases this figure went up to 60 partners in the same period. Only seven per cent reported using condoms as a protection against AIDS. The target population was aware of the existence of AIDS but had very little knowledge of its transmission modes and prevention techniques and methods. The research showed clearly the need for a vigorous AIDS education campaign through every possible method of communication.

PLANNING

The programme was funded by United States based Family Health International through AIDSTECH. Once funding had been secured, activity sites were identified at appropriate operational centres along the main highways which link Kenya, Tanzania, Zambia and Malawi. The sites were selected on the basis of the target population present. These sites are frequented by truck drivers and their assistants and consequently the centres attract scores of women who engage in promiscuity with the truckers. This predisposes them to the threat of HIV infection. The sites are situated in such a way that the distances between them are long enough to ensure that if a driver bypasses one centre he is bound to stop at the next one.

The intervention programme was planned to help the target population understand how AIDS and STDs can be prevented, and to encourage them to adopt safer sex practices, eg by reducing the number of sexual partners and using condoms as a preventive measure.

IMPLEMENTATION

The AIDS intervention activities of AMREF are vetted by government established AIDS coordinating bodies. AMREF submitted their proposals separately to Kenya and Tanzania. Immediate clearance was received and support was enlisted from relevant formal and informal leaders and groups. Seminars and workshops were held for these leaders. The business community was informed about the objectives of the programme before activities were started at the truck stops. This careful approach gave the programme a broad base and a community identity which guaranteed continuity and sustainability.

Owing to the high mobility of truck drivers, their assistants and their sexual partners, they tend to engage in multiple and unprotected sexual contact, creating a major risk of the rapid spread of HIV infection. A change to safer sex was therefore absolutely essential to reduce the risks of infection and to control the spread of the virus.

A wide range of appropriate educational and communication strategies were adopted and put into practice. The strategies employed include one-to-one communication of AIDS messages by trained peer educators; displaying posters, car stickers, ashtrays, T-shirts and key chains as giveaways; video shows; pop music; focused messages and explanatory brochures. To respond to the demand created by education and communication, condoms were made available through free condom dispensers at bars and lodges.

EVALUATION

Local and international media have covered the intervention programme very extensively. This has been valuable in strengthening official and non-official support for the campaign.

The actual evaluation of the programme, however, must be an assessment of the extent to which the spread of the disease has been contained and reduced. This evaluation is carried out through trip reports and reports from peer educators.

On average, 250,000 condoms are being distributed every month. There is a significant adoption of safer sex practices. For instance, the demand for condoms has increased steadily and interviews with field sex workers indicate that they have been witnessing a reduction in the number of different sexual partners. The governments have become more and more involved and are contributing to the programme in terms of specialised experts, the supply of condoms and general support.

Following AMREF's initiatives along the Trans-Africa Highway in Kenya and the Dar es Salaam—Tunduma Highway, similar activities are mushrooming on a smaller scale in the region. Examples of such activities include the Thwake Truck Drivers AIDS project in Kenya; the barmaids and commercial sex workers project in Kisumu, Kenya and the Truck Drivers AIDS project in Iringa in Tanzania. All these projects have expanded tremendously during the first six months of 1992. AMREF have supplied details of numerous sites where positive action similar to that described earlier in this report is helping to contain this health problem. It is too early to claim success in this programme but the authorities and the aid agencies are now fully alerted to the magnitude of the threat to the whole country if this spread of contagion is not contained. AMREF is now largely playing the role of an umbrella coordinator today.

CASE DISCUSSION

Some observers decry public relations as largely irrelevant, others expect it to work miracles. If ever a miracle were possible, this situation in Kenya and Tanzania demands it. Great credit is due to AMREF, who having researched and identified the frightening scale of the problem has taken the initiative to try to contain its worst excesses and to bring sex education and information about AIDS to a section of the African population which is rushing headlong into disaster.

This case has several interesting features:

- The extent of the problem was identified by appropriate research.
- Funding was secured.
- The governments were alerted to the magnitude of the emergency.
- As wide as possible support was gathered together to support the initiatives. The media were used to gain maximum publicity for the need to pursue the campaign of education and communication energetically.
- The actual interface between educators and those requiring counsel and guidance had to be carried out on the sites which had been established on many different African highways.

Case 7.4 A suitable case for treatment

BACKGROUND

The State Hospital, Carstairs, Lanarkshire, Scotland is a secure psychiatric hospital serving the needs of patients from Scotland and Northern Ireland.

Considered by many as a home for the 'maddest and the baddest in the land' for more than four decades, the State Hospital had a reputation as the place where the most violent, dangerous, criminal psychopaths were sent and locked away for ever.

In 1976, when the hospital was still part of the Prison Service, two prisoners escaped and killed three people with axes. These murders are part of the legend and history that TMA Communications Limited of Glasgow were asked to change.

A number of changes have resulted at the State Hospital, following the introduction of the 1984 Mental Health (Scotland) Act, the introduction of new management in 1989, and the government's edict assimilating the State Hospital from the Prison Service into the National Health Service.

As a result, TMA Communications were briefed to introduce a media relations programme, and a community and professional communication programme which would challenge the public misconception of the role of the State Hospital, and to change the image and legend it represented.

RESEARCH

Initial research revealed very early on that there were, in addition to external problems, major internal problems. Until 1989, as part of the Prison Service, the regime within the hospital had been one of custody, control and restraint.

With the introduction of new management procedures, the treatment methods changed to those of patient care and therapy. This, in turn lead to dissension on the part of many of the hospital's employees who were accustomed to the traditional prison service approach – that if you misbehaved, you were constrained and put into isolation.

157

Today, patients are now sent to the State Hospital for treatment, not detention or retention. Once treatment is considered to have been completed, they are returned to other institutions, prisons, hospitals or the community.

Other problems were ongoing accusations by a number of employees who wished to stop the changes by providing headlines for newspapers.

While TMA Communications were not qualified to enter into debate regarding the methods of patient treatment, it was clear that the hospital had dedicated professional staff, who understood clearly what the differences were, and why and how patients should be treated.

Research showed clearly that there were many interesting challenges to be faced.

PLANNING

In close cooperation with the management, the following seven main objectives of the programme were agreed:

1. To change public perception and understanding of the new role of the State Hospital within the National Health Service.
2. To encourage participation on the part of employees in the development of professional services and improved standards of nursing care for patients.
3. To challenge head-on any criticism from whatever quarter – the media, staff, local community, etc.
4. To create an awareness of therapy and care for patients as opposed to custody and control of prisoners.
5. To establish a better understanding between the hospital, the professional clinicians at the hospital and their counterparts within the NHS and local health authorities.
6. To create among the staff and professional members of the hospital a sense of pride from working at the hospital and a recognition of their achievements in mental health care which are being practised within the establishment.
7. To promote human rights for patients rather than for prisoners.

Public relations strategy

The agreed objectives would obviously need careful strategic planning and the requirements were listed under nine headings:

1. Adopt an open-door policy to the media.
2. Challenge vigorously any misrepresentation in the media.
3. Produce and publicise a Patient's Charter.
4. Produce an Employees' and Communications Charter.
5. Produce a Security Charter.
6. Encourage proactive response by the media to initiatives undertaken by the hospital as far as its professional clinical achievements were concerned.
7. Adopt an up-front direct response to any crisis issue.
8. Implement a programme of media training for the management, reviewed every six months.
9. Review a number of options such as changing the name, introducing a staff newsletter, etc.

The options under heading 9 were rejected and instead a series of 48 presentations were made to small groups from the 500 staff members explaining the Vision, the Mission and the new objectives of the State Hospital.

Similar presentations were also made to local health authorities, local GPs, and members of the judiciary and police, indicating the level of services now available at the State Hospital.

Identification of the publics

Many of the target publics had been identified in the objectives and strategy. The key action that was promoted, and continues to be promoted, is one of an open policy. Every enquiry, every complaint, every issue, is dealt with in an immediate and open fashion. Whatever the complaint — for example criticism against staff, an incident at the hospital, the introduction of new policies — there is an open door. At no time in the past four years has the hospital closed its doors on a media enquiry.

Given the special nature of the hospital and its patients, there are occasions when the hospital is unable to pass comment on either individual patients or their treatment. That does not preclude discussion in general terms but it does afford a certain protection.

Selection of media

Within the general public media there are two categories: the sensationalist and the serious. As part of the policy of the open communication programme, it was necessary to take the good with the bad. It was possible, however, to try to be selective in some of the information distributed to certain publications.

Invariably, media enquiries were responded to immediately. When statements were being prepared on specific subjects, it was often necessary to arrange private briefings with key journalists.

Budget

The public relations budget for the year was £40,000. This included the consultancy fee, print production and photography.

IMPLEMENTATION

Meetings were arranged with identified specialist writers dealing with health issues in Scotland, including television, radio and the press.

Individual briefings were arranged for these journalists at which the General Manager, Director of Nurses and Director of Medicines met the journalists and briefed them on the change of philosophy and purposes of the hospital.

During the year, many new services were introduced at the hospital and these were publicised. They included:

- the end of slopping out;
- introduction of mixed sex wards;
- ground parole;
- occupational therapy development;
- the sale of goods produced within the hospital;
- the expansion of nursing services;
- a conference established for NHS managers and executives together with members of the judiciary, police and local authorities.

The State Hospital maintained regular weekly contact with the media throughout the year. A number of issues arose for attention, including challenges from the Staff Prison Officers Association (SPOA), incidents within the hospital and the introduction of the new regimes mentioned above.

Press releases, press briefings and media visits have all formed part of the media relations programme. The scope of this audience has been broadened from medical writers to include women and other feature writers. Television and radio journalists have visited the hospital to improve their understanding and to learn that the hospital is more than willing to address issues.

On the crisis management side, a running battle has been fought with the SPOA but the SPOA finally declared peace, acknowledging that after 12 months of challenge, counter-challenge and defeat, they were not winning any medals.

One other crisis occurred when a training nurse had her throat cut. An immediate announcement was issued to the media, announcing the setting up of an internal review. This was followed by a press conference at which the results of the internal review were made available to the media. All this occurred within 14 days of the incident.

Challenges concerning consultants leaving the hospital were handled appropriately, bearing in mind that any circumstantial activity that could prejudice the view of the hospital is pounced upon by certain elements of the media.

A formal crisis management programme was developed and implemented.

EVALUATION

It had been recognised by the management that the programme to change the attitude to the State Hospital would have to be a long-term commitment. However, the openness of the management in welcoming enquiries from the media and addressing them efficiently has gone a long way to changing the historic practice of attacking the hospital to one of enquiry, investigation and interview.

There is a long way to go before all the agreed objectives can be achieved but the following aims have been realised:

- The media now clearly recognise that significant changes have taken place and are continuing.
- The management and the staff are committed to patients' rehabilitation as opposed to the old regime of confinement and constraint.
- Families are responding positively to the introduction of the Patient's Charter. They are now engaged in open dialogue with the clinicians who are prepared to discuss elements of treatment for the patients and look at short-term rehabilitation and development, rather than long-term incarceration.

Imitation is a sincere form of flattery. Following a recent enquiry into Ashworth Hospital, a similar psychiatric hospital in England, the policies adopted and practised at the State Hospital in Scotland have been used as a blueprint for any future development in special hospitals in England and Wales.

Members of the National Health Service, the judiciary and

prisons are now very clearly aware of the level of professional services available to them.

CASE DISCUSSION

This report emphasises, once again, that public relations theory and practice can make a great improvement in the most unlikely circumstances. Tony Meehan and his team at TMA Communications are to be commended for accepting this formidable challenge. This view was shared by the IPRA International Jury which gave the 1994 overall Golden World Award of excellence to this case study out of the 143 entries submitted from 29 different countries.

This campaign succeeded in informing both public and staff about a new therapeutic approach aimed at rehabilitation rather than custody. As a result, the policies adopted and practised by the State Hospital in Scotland are being used as a blueprint for future development in special hospitals in England and Wales.

The 1993–94 annual report of the hospital is deservedly proud of what has been achieved. It refers to the success of the hospital's charters and expresses considerable satisfaction that the hospital was awarded the government's prestigious Charter Mark on 17 October 1994 for its continuous excellence of service. The State Hospital was one of the very few Scottish public service organisations given this award in 1994.

Another distinction with which the hospital can be pleased was the achievement of BS 5750 Part 1, the BSI Registration Award for quality standards. The State Hospital is the first NHS hospital in the UK to achieve BS 5750 certification.

This example of a public relations consultancy working closely with top management to achieve rather ambitious objectives in a distinctly hostile environment should be brought to the attention of those critics of the public relations profession who claim that public relations is merely cosmetic and often a barrier to the truth.

Case 7.5 Hazards of pre- and post-natal smoking

BACKGROUND

This case study describes one campaign of the Victorian Smoking and Health Programme which is a joint initiative of the Anti-Cancer Council of Australia, the Department of Health and Community Services and the National Heart Foundation. It is supported substantially with funds from the Victorian Health Promotion Foundation. The 'Quit' logo is a registered trade mark of the Anti-Cancer Council of Victoria. We are indebted to Yolanda Reid, Manager of Professional Education and Information Services, for this report on the special Quit programme Pre- and Post-Natal Campaign which won a Golden World Award in the IPRA competition.

In Australia, 30 per cent of pregnant women are smokers. Only one in five stop or cut down their smoking during their pregnancy and approximately 60 per cent of these women start smoking again after the birth of their child. It is now medically well-established that smokers have a greater risk of miscarriage and many have complications during the birth. A baby born to a smoker is more likely to be underweight and therefore more vulnerable to infection and other health problems. Babies and children subjected to passive smoking are more likely to develop asthma and other respiratory problems.

The Victorian Smoking and Health Programme (Quit Campaign) in its role of reducing the prevalence of smoking in Victoria, Australia saw the need to develop a health education programme targeted at encouraging pregnant women who smoke to quit. For its success, the programme needed to be developed in consultation and collaboration with health professionals working in the pre- and post-natal areas. This included major health professional associations, maternal and child-care associations and hospitals.

RESEARCH

Field visits to pre-natal and maternity clinics revealed that messages given to women about quitting smoking were inconsistent.

Sometimes women were advised to quit, on other occasions they were advised only to cut down. This confused women and gave them a good excuse for not making a decision to quit.

While health professionals were fully aware of the dangers of smoking during pregnancy, they only related this to the baby's health. One of the main messages that pregnant women needed to hear was that both their own health and the health of the baby were important. Pregnant women also had limited understanding of the harmful effects of passive smoking.

An extensive literature review was undertaken of studies on smoking and pregnancy, post-partum relapse, passive smoking and health professionals counselling smoking patients. Existing pre- and post-natal programmes in Australia and internationally were also reviewed.

Because health professionals have influence over patients, it was decided to develop an integrated programme through their professional associations to tackle the issue in a structured manner.

Research indicated that in addition to printed resources a short video dealing with the effects of smoking during pregnancy would be valuable in pre-natal clinics. In addition, it was clear that any resources produced for health professionals would be most useful if presented in the form of a small free-standing display.

Pre-testing was carried out to determine the most appropriate messages and communication that would influence women and also encourage the support of health professionals.

PLANNING

The objectives of the programme were threefold:

1. To raise the awareness of pregnant women who smoke of the risks of smoking to their babies and themselves.
2. To increase the awareness of parents and families of the dangers of passive smoking, particularly to babies and young children.
3. To obtain the support, endorsement and continuing involvement of health professionals working in the pre- and post-natal areas.

Target publics

The priority publics were identified under four headings:

1. pregnant women who smoke;

2. partners of pregnant women who smoke;
3. parents who smoke;
4. health professionals and carers working in pre- and post-natal areas, eg obstetricians and gynaecologists, midwives and paediatricians.

The success of the programme would be measured on:

- an increase in awareness of the dangers of smoking during and after pregnancy and around children;
- an increase in the activity of health professionals in counselling patients and handing out information.

Communication strategies

The strategy adopted was to provide clear information on the dangers of smoking and to offer assistance to those wanting to quit. The intention of the programme was not to alienate and anger the target groups but to present facts in a positive and caring form without being guilt inducing.

Themes

The programme's main messages were:

- Smoking during pregnancy is dangerous to both the baby and the mother.
- Passive smoking is particularly dangerous to young children.
- Quitting *is* possible and there is help available.

The chosen approach needed to be sympathetic and relevant to women. Research had indicated that the most effective messages should be:

- clear and believable and presented in a positive, non-judgmental way;
- supported by strong, positive and captivating images related to pregnancy, children and parents.

Techniques

The central communication tool developed was a series of attractive brochures held in a display stand. Four brochures were produced:

- *Smoking and Pregnancy;*
- *Staying stopped. Remaining a non-smoker after your pregnancy;*

- *Passive smoking and your children;*
- *How to help the pregnant mother to quit; a guide for health professionals.*

The texts of the brochures were approved by health professionals and the concepts pre-tested with target audiences.

Obtaining endorsements

Twelve organisations were approached to endorse formally the programme to give it credibility. They were:

- The Asthma Foundation of Victoria;
- Australian College of Midwives Inc − Victoria Branch;
- The Australian College of Paediatricians;
- Australian Lactation Consultants Association;
- Australian Physiotherapy Association − Women's Health Group, Victorian Chapter;
- Mercy Hospital for Women;
- National Asthma Campaign;
- Nursing Mothers' Association of Australia;
- Royal Children's Hospital;
- The Victorian State Committee of the Royal Australian College of Obstetricians and Gynaecologists;
- The Royal Victorian Eye and Ear Hospital;
- The Royal Women's Hospital.

All these bodies promoted the programme through their newsletters and distributed material to their members.

Other resource material

To encourage attitude and behavioural change, other communication tools were produced to support the messages in the brochures. These were:

For women

1. Two attractive posters − dealing with pregnancy and smoking and passive smoking − for use in health professionals' waiting rooms, hospitals, maternal and child health centres and community health centres. Three versions of the passive smoking poster covered 12 language groups.
2. A video titled 'Baby Breathing' for screening in pre-natal classes. This was produced in response to a need identified by midwives.

3. A Quit farmyard mobile for the baby's room with the message: 'Please don't smoke — baby breathing'. This was intended as a non-confrontational way of asking family and friends not to smoke near their baby.
4. Maternity T-shirts with the message 'Please don't smoke, baby breathing' and children's T-shirts with the message 'Kid's lungs at work, please don't smoke'. This was intended as a subtle way of asking people not to smoke.
5. A series of baby's and children's stickers with non-smoking messages for baby's and children's rooms, prams, skateboards and school books.
6. Advertisements in national parents' and women's magazines and on Melbourne trams. Both posters were used as advertisements to promote further the dangers of smoking.

For health professionals

A guide on how to counsel pregnant smokers — research had shown that many health professionals lacked the skill to counsel their patients about their smoking and therefore a simple and easy-to-use guide was produced and distributed.

Budget

A budget of A$270,000 was made available for the development and implementation of the programme. This included resource production, pre-testing of messages, additional production costs and advertising. Of this total, A$10,000 was spent on public relations and A$40,000 on advertising.

IMPLEMENTATION

The launch

The programme was launched at a major women's hospital and it was attended by health professional colleges, associations and agencies and the media. A well-known Australian actress and singer, Jane Clifton, who was six months pregnant with her second child, hosted the event. Representatives from Quit, the Royal College of Obstetricians and Gynaecologists, the Mercy Hospital for Women and the Royal Women's Hospital delivered speeches and commended the programme.

The launch featured the baby whose photograph appeared in the brochure and on the posters, plus 12 newly born babies and many others. They were all wearing the T-shirts with the message 'Please don't smoke, baby breathing'.

The launch achieved the following results:

- coverage in the evening news of two TV stations;
- mention in most news bulletins;
- 18 media interviews;
- a photograph and a full story on the front page of Melbourne's leading newspaper, *The Age*;
- coverage in the print media statewide;
- coverage in all the medical journals.

Supporting publicity and advertising

Editorial was secured in leading parenting and women's magazines. In each case, the text of the women's brochures was published unchanged. Editorial also appeared in health promotion agency magazines.

The pregnancy poster: 'Can you think of a better reason to quit smoking' and the passive smoking poster: 'Everyone at this table is smoking' were placed in several baby and parent magazines and on 530 Melbourne trams.

The brochure series proved so successful among the target group that a television commercial was produced based on the text of the *Passive smoking and your children* brochure and promoted a 'Welcome to our Smoke Free Home' sticker.

It was estimated that during the campaign period at least 90 per cent of Victorian families would have seen the advertisements at least five times. The advertisement was screened on all commercial TV stations during the campaign period and is now being shown on closed circuit television in public hospitals. In one year, it will have been screened 520,390 times.

Direct mail

The programme material was mailed to:

- the 12 sponsoring bodies for them to distribute;
- 120 local community health centres;
- maternity and pre-natal clinics in metropolitan and rural hospitals;
- 800 maternal and child health centres;
- 200 child-care centres;
- 1200 kindergartens;
- 15 Quit Rural Resource Centres;

- 4000 general medical practitioners, with a special promotion of the material.

The widespread publicity also created a direct demand and altogether 310,000 brochures were distributed in five months.

Promotion at conferences

Papers were presented at national and international health promotion and medical conferences describing the process of developing the programme thereby promoting greater awareness of it among health professionals and workers in tobacco controlled organisations.

Hospital open days and community-based promotions

The programme materials were promoted at hospital open days, community festivals and special concerts sponsored by Quit. For example, at the Children's Performance Arena at a major country folk festival, the stage area was dressed with Quit banners, passive smoking posters and mobiles. Quit T-shirts and mobiles were given away as prizes for parents and children. The 10,000 copies of the official programme carried a Quit advertisement. Also an information stand and the programme materials were promoted at 15 Humphrey B Bear concerts attended by families.

'Quit week' promotion with passive smoking theme

The 1992 Quit Week involved the participation of all the extensive Quit networks. Hospitals, doctors, community health centres, health promotion agencies, maternal and child-care centres, kindergartens, schools and many others helped to promote the message of the effect of passive smoking on children. A media event launched Quit Week and the passive smoking television commercial. Results achieved were:

- coverage on the evening news of four TV stations;
- mention on main news bulletins and 20 interviews on radio;
- extensive coverage in newspapers statewide – 116 press items.

EVALUATION

In order to measure response to the programme, semi-structured interviews were conducted with key health professionals who had been using the campaign's materials. The aims of these interviews were:

- to assess professional response to the campaign materials in community health centres and hospitals;
- to assess the perceived usefulness of the materials and the way they were used.

In order to do this, interviews were conducted at 18 hospital maternity clinics and 13 community health centres. In the maternity clinics, a senior midwife was interviewed, usually the nurse-in-charge or the nurse educator.

Hospitals

There was a high level of awareness of the brochures, and *Smoking and Pregnancy*, *Staying stopped* and *Passive smoking and your children* were displayed, given to patients or both in 16 hospitals. The least used item was the video, which was only used in five hospitals. Overall, the interviewees responded very favourably to the programme materials, praising their professionalism, convenience, visual appeal and content. The only critical comment was that the items may not be suitable for pregnant teenagers, a large proportion of whom smoke.

Community health centres

The community health centres approached were a random sample of those known to have ordered pre- and post-natal resources at least once. The centres had a wide diversity of clientele, needs, staffing, facilities, affluence and size, which made a large difference to their reaction. All the interviewees found the material well presented, colourful and informative but those working with clients in poor economic circumstances found them too 'middle class'. In their opinion, the images in the brochures were not appropriate for some clients, particularly teenage mothers.

CASE DISCUSSION

The case study was well referenced with details of all the research papers and reports which had been used to produce the brochures and other materials. They have been omitted from this case study as they do not add anything to the details of the public relations programme.

This problem is not confined to Australia but appears to be more serious there than in many other countries. This report shows the value of seeking endorsement and support from all the many different interests concerned about the prevalence of smoking by mothers and in the home where there are small children.

In the UK, a report has been issued recently describing a very large research project into the relationship of smoking to cot deaths. The danger of a cot death is much greater if the mother is a smoker or if the baby is in a smoking environment. This is perhaps a subject which Quit can include in their future programmes.

The comment on the reduced relevance of the programme to pregnant teenagers and teenage mothers points to the difficulty of using the same arguments and material to influence different age and economic groups. Perhaps the answer is to adapt the general message to appeal to specific groups.

Case 7.6 Promoting organ donation in Israel

BACKGROUND

Modern surgery has been able to perform miracles with organ transplants but the problem is securing an adequate supply of suitable organs from donors. This is a problem in most countries and is particularly acute in Israel. The Israel Ministry of Health decided to mount a public relations campaign in Israel to publicise the need for public support and asked Logos Mass Communications of Tel Aviv to prepare a scheme.

RESEARCH

Before actively planning and designing a campaign, the agency surveyed doctors, nurses, patients and social workers about the problems of obtaining suitable organs for transplant. This research was carried out through personal meetings with relevant medical and social workers and transplant recipients and their families. Careful attention was also paid to reports which had been prepared by doctors and social workers about their experiences when contacting the families of suitable donors and in some cases the potential donors themselves.

The survey revealed that reservations concerning organ donation were universal in Israel, cutting across all socio-economic groups, including the highly educated and top income groups. The research indicated that the reasons for these reservations were complex, incorporating a mix of religious, ideological and personal elements that included fear with regard to the fate of one's body and a deep-rooted worry that one might not receive all the proper medical attention needed if one had previously indicated a willingness to donate an organ.

It became evident from the research that to overcome this negative attitude towards organ donation it would not be sufficient to present appeals from members of the medical community who were regarded as interested parties. A combined effort would be necessary by such accepted leaders as politicians, legislators, educators, clerics and public personalities.

A steering committee was set up to assess the local research and to compare it with reports from various public transplant organisations in the US, UK and Belgium, as well as the European Centre for Transplants in the Netherlands. The steering committee comprised representatives of the Israel Ministry of Health, five senior physicians specialising in the transplant of kidneys, hearts, livers and corneas, and a representative of the agency, Logos Mass Communications. The agreed conclusions reached by the steering committee served as the basis for planning the campaign.

PLANNING

It should be noted that the idea for the need of such a campaign originated with the agency which had presented a preliminary proposal to the Ministry of Health. This set out reasons for mounting such a campaign, describing how it would work in general terms and estimating the costs. After securing the agreement of the Ministry, the research described above was carried out and based on this the final design and planning of the programme was conducted.

The concept

The campaign was conceived as a broad, comprehensive public relations effort targeted at as wide a cross-section of the public as possible. It aimed at achieving maximum multimedia exposure through clear and direct information about all the aspects of the subject, even the most sensitive points.

A slogan, a very catchy rhyme in Hebrew, was created and it was used on all printed matter and used at all events. An approximate translation of the slogan is: 'donating organs grants life'.

All relevant persons and interested sectors were mobilised to convey the message. The target publics for the campaign included the Minister of Health and top officials in the Ministry, legislators, politicians, educators, clerics, public personalities, doctors, nurses, social workers, transplant recipients, patients waiting for transplants and members of their families.

The message

Seven major messages were developed:

1. Organ transplant is the only way to save the lives of thousands of people.
2. The medical community world-wide, and in Israel, is able to carry out successfully many types of transplants.
3. Organ transplant in Israel is possible only if organs are donated, usually by members of the patient's family.
4. The decision to donate must be taken at a tragic moment and must be quick and decisive.
5. A signed pre-agreement by a potential donor frees the donor's family from making a difficult decision.
6. Recent developments have reduced the possibility of acquiring organs from foreign organ banks, making local donation essential.
7. There are no Jewish, Muslim or Christian religious restrictions against organ donation.

IMPLEMENTATION

The slogan which had been developed was used to give cohesion to the printed materials and special events which were developed during the campaign. The following print/electronic media items, all backed up by the slogan, were executed:

- Prior to and during the campaign, the print and electronic media were bombarded with numerous press releases. The usage of this material was very high.
- A 30-second TV spot, featuring a 12-year-old male kidney transplant recipient, was broadcast on Israel's three TV channels 20 times during the campaign.
- A 30-second radio spot was broadcast on most of Israel's radio channels one hundred times during the campaign.
- Two posters were designed, featuring two transplant recipients; the young man with the kidney transplant and a 43-year-old male heart transplant recipient. The posters were hung in hospitals, community centres, health fund clinics, high schools and municipal poster sites in 30 different towns.
- A two-colour flyer was produced in Hebrew and Arabic versions, explaining the need for donating organs and how to donate an organ, and included a donation agreement form to be completed and returned by mail. These were distributed in tens of thousands throughout the country.
- Car stickers, featuring the slogan, were distributed to thousands of hospital personnel, patients and their visitors.

- Advertisements appeared throughout the month in Hebrew, Arabic and English language daily newspapers.

Special events were organised, all of which received extensive coverage in the print and electronic media. These included:

- A one-day seminar for health and medical journalists from all the media was held several days prior to the official launching of the campaign. Explanations of all aspects of the subject were presented by medical, sociological, psychological and legal experts.
- The opening ceremony of the campaign was held in the Knesset under the auspices of the Speaker of the House and the Minister of Health. The ceremony was attended by transplant recipients and their families, medical and social workers and members of the Knesset.
- A public symposium was held on organ transplant and donation in conjunction with Tel Aviv University with a panel including a senior medical specialist, a law professor, the Chief Rabbi of North Tel Aviv and the Minister of Health. About 450 people attended this symposium.
- A meeting in a large Tel Aviv public hall was attended by 200 transplant recipients from all over the country and 100 members of the medical community, social workers, municipal leaders and the Minister of Health. The meeting was addressed by a leading surgeon and the first Israeli heart transplant recipient.

EVALUATION

The campaign successfully placed before the whole country the subject of organ transplant and donation, including a persuasive professional discussion of its importance and the problems involved. It was instrumental in lifting the veil of secrecy, and to a certain extent the shame, which had obfuscated the entire subject of transplant recipients of all types, thereby legitimising their position and needs. The campaign was also successful in displaying an important and impressive aspect of Israel's medical capability. In terms of quantitative success, several thousand persons submitted completed organ donor pre-agreement forms.

Disappointingly, the campaign did not sufficiently emphasise the international aspect of the subject as the planned international symposium did not take place. The agency was also not successful in gaining the cooperation of the military, which would have added an important dimension to the campaign.

The agency's recommendations for the future included a low-key, carefully planned, constant and continuing campaign, culminating with an annual 10 to 14-day high profile campaign which would ensure that the subject would be kept on the public agenda. The agency also recommended that in order to reach new immigrants the languages of the campaign should be broadened to include Russian, and perhaps Spanish, while outreach should be extended to the high school population and military personnel. A final recommendation was that a data bank on various transplant cases be created to serve as an information reserve for future publicity events.

CASE DISCUSSION

This case study demonstrates the constraints which hinder the development of a vital health resource. The clinical need for the donation of organs to use in transplantation is well accepted but this does not help with the difficulty of obtaining suitable donations. The answer to this dilemma is a positive public relations programme directed, on the one hand, to publicise the urgent need for donations and on the other hand to do everything possible to meet relatives' natural reluctance to give permission for this.

Case 7.7 'The Educated Stomach'

BACKGROUND

A Vitamin Information Service (VIS) is operated throughout the world by Hoffman La Roche. It is a generic service offering information on vitamins and their role in promoting good health. In the United Kingdom the VIS is designed for use by health care professionals and the media, both of whom play a key role in educating the consumer.

The VIS answers specific queries from health care professionals and the media on vitamins and nutrition, and produces leaflets and other literature on areas of interest and development. An independent Scientific Advisory Group monitors and approves all information issued by the Vitamin Information Service.

'The Educated Stomach' was a research project carried out during 1990 by Countrywide Communications (London) who were the retained public relations consultancy to Hoffman La Roche for the Vitamin Information Service. This research project formed a major element in the public relations programme which Countrywide implemented for the VIS in 1990.

RESEARCH

As part of the Vitamin Information Service's desire to contact high risk groups, Countrywide undertook a research project into the dietary habits of first-year male students in self-catering accommodation. Most of these students were making their first attempt to manage their diet outside the discipline and budget of the family home. Due to their inexperience in shopping and cooking, and the lack of structured family meals, this group was perceived to be high risk — that is, potentially vulnerable to vitamin deficiency.

The research was designed with the following objectives:

1. to investigate the cooking and shopping habits of male students during their first year at university;

2. to ascertain what changes had taken place in their eating habits since leaving home;
3. to assess their level of knowledge on what constituted a healthy diet and to examine their attitudes and behaviour towards current food and health issues.

PLANNING

The results of the research were used to achieve the following objectives for the Vitamin Information Service in 1990:

●   to promote awareness of the benefits of vitamins with regard to 'high risk' groups. A high risk group is identified as those who may require extra vitamins, such as children or pregnant mothers, or anyone who may not be eating a carefully balanced diet due to illness or unwise lifestyle;

●   to increase awareness of the Vitamin Information Service among health professionals, the health care and consumer media, and consumers via the two former groups.

●   to establish the Vitamin Information Service as the automatic point of contact in the United Kingdom for media requiring information on vitamins and nutrition;

●   to establish the Vitamin Information Service as an authoritative source of material on vitamins and nutrition for health professionals and the media.

IMPLEMENTATION

To be scientifically credible, the research had to be quantitative. However, a qualitative dimension was additionally needed to provide the desired material as a basis for writing interesting media stories. The execution was as follows:

●   Execution of research by the internationally regarded nutrition department of Queen Margaret College, Edinburgh.

●   A detailed dietary questionnaire was compiled in conjunction with the Scientific Group and sent to 700 first-year male students in six selected universities in England, Scotland and Wales.

●   The results of the questionnaire were analysed by Queen Margaret College and the Scientific Advisory Group.

●   A series of small group interviews were arranged with student volunteers at three of the selected universities in order to examine dietary attitudes.

- The results of the survey were used to compile an illustrated report titled 'The Educated Stomach'.
- The main findings of the research were used to produce press releases closely targeted to individual media.
- The report, accompanied by customised press releases, was sent to the national press, radio and television; the regional press, radio and television; and the health professional media.

The releases were timed to reach the press at the height of the student examination period in June. The students taking part in the survey were just finishing their first year at university and media interest in the general area of graduate education was high. A second batch of releases was issued in September to coincide with media articles about first year students starting at university.

The publication 'The Educated Stomach' was subtitled 'a report on the eating habits of first-year male university students'. It was excellently produced and illustrated with humorous drawings (see Figure 13).

Some of the findings in the report are worth quoting.

Most students in fact led a fairly healthy lifestyle. 85 per cent did not smoke; 64 per cent exercised regularly; 35 per cent did not drink or drank less than 10 units of alcohol per week, equivalent to 5 pints of beer; 46 per cent of students took

Figure 13 One of the illustrations from 'The Educated Stomach'

vitamin supplements; only 7 per cent of students were heavy drinkers.

The report concluded with a prophecy of what a student will be like in the year 2000.

> On average, he is likely to be more healthy than his predecessors, much more aware of advice on healthy lifestyles. From his interest in food, he is likely to be choosier about the taste, quality and nutritional value of what he is buying and eating. Even with the greater range of easily prepared foods, he will also be more competent in the kitchen and will enjoy cooking.

EVALUATION

Hoffman La Roche were very satisfied with the results of the exercise which included the following:

1. Awareness of the Vitamin Information Service was increased as a result of the media coverage of the survey which appeared in a total of 27 print media and 27 broadcast media. The Vitamin Information Service's name achieved a rating of 20,104,780 opportunities to see by the target audience (total print and broadcast reach);

2. The research helped to promote the awareness of the benefits of vitamins with regard to 'high risk' groups by revealing that nearly half the students took vitamin supplements as 'insurance' against an unhealthy diet. This was widely reported in the media;

3. Enquiries to the Vitamin Information Service from health professionals and the media rose significantly as a result of the survey.

4. The survey helped to establish the credibility and authority of the VIS among health professionals and the media by its execution and preservation as a fully scientific project yielding statistically significant results. The help and endorsement of the Scientific Advisory Group, and the involvement of Queen Margaret College was also a crucial element in the recognition of the survey as a scientifically sound document.

5. The survey generated a high proportion of positive messages about vitamins. The press cuttings were rated according to the degree of positiveness towards the survey and vitamins and the importance of the media covering the survey. The average rating scored 'excellent'.

The total cost of the research, including all fees and disbursements, was £25,000.

CASE DISCUSSION

There are a number of noteworthy aspects of this case study. The name of the sponsoring company, Hoffman La Roche, is clearly associated with the activities of the Vitamin Information Service and with the survey which formed the core of this particular campaign. In the past, there have been some instances where companies have used 'front organisations' with impressive names which suggest they are official or objective in their recommendations whereas they have been operating for the benefit of a particular, but unnamed, sponsor. Members of the Institute of Public Relations are expressly forbidden by their code of professional conduct from having anything to do with 'front organisations'.

These strictures do not apply to the case in question. Most people would appreciate that a Vitamin Information Service is probably keen to sell more vitamins for its parent company. This makes it very important to find imaginative ways of attracting media and customer attention to the product. The idea of concentrating on high risk groups is sound marketing but ingenuity is required to find suitable avenues for bringing the attention of the media and their readers to a subject which is not intrinsically newsworthy.

This campaign relied for its success on a carefully orchestrated series of events. First, choosing first-year male university students as the subject of the survey at a time when university education was attracting much interest from the general public. Then deciding on a survey and producing a suitable questionnaire with the help of Queen Margaret College, Edinburgh and its Scientific Group, thus establishing its credibility. The choice of a distinctive title 'The Educated Stomach' and the inclusion of a set of excellent cartoons in the published report undoubtedly helped to lift this particular subject out of the mass of communications which bombard the editorial offices.

The timing of both the issuance of the questionnaires and the publication of the report were critical for the success of the whole programme. The agency also went to the trouble of issuing customised press releases to accompany the reports. The campaign deserved to succeed, and it is encouraging to see such a very professionally planned operation reaching its clearly defined objectives.

8

Business to Business

Case 8.1 The Lion Mark for safety and quality

BACKGROUND

In the past, many children have suffered injury, or even death, from toys which were attractive but potentially lethal. 'Horror stories' had become a regular feature of the pre-Christmas toy buying season. Typical newspaper headlines were:

'Toys that can kill or maim'
'Hazardous tots' toys'
'Safety chief issues killer toy warning'
'Toy puppet alarm'
'Perilous toys'

Members of the British Toy and Hobby Manufacturers Association (BTHA), the representative body of the British Toy Industry, were increasingly concerned about the poor image of their £1000 million industry. It was therefore decided in 1987 to seek the advice of public relations consultants, GCI Sterling.

RESEARCH

The BTHA asked GCI Sterling to research and analyse the causes of the industry's image problems and to take corrective action. The BTHA knew that its safety record was the best in the world and that it had cooperated with the British Standards Institute (BSI) to create safety standards. These standards are adhered to by all its members and were adopted by the EEC as the cornerstone of the new CE Safety Regulations. The BTHA were convinced that its members were being unfairly pilloried by the media, and that the new IBA advertising restrictions were a direct result of this.

The first step taken by GCI Sterling was to commission a MORI survey to find out exactly what the public and its representatives felt about the British Toy Industry and its products. This survey investigated the attitudes of mothers, members of Parliament, trading standards officers and the national, regional and local media.

The results of the survey showed clearly that safety was top of the agenda, both as a concern and as the area where parents and legislators believed the toy industry was falling short of their expectations for purely mercenary reasons. The survey also revealed that, by and large, toys were regarded as an expensive and irritating purchase, both trivial and valueless. (Perhaps children might have voiced a different opinion!)

PLANNING

Based on the research findings, the BTHA and their consultants agreed a strategy based on immediate corrective action on the toy safety question where the truth was so widely divergent from the public perception. It was also to embark on a longer term programme to emphasise the value of play in the development of children's imaginative and social abilities.

The early introduction of a recognisable safety symbol was agreed as the proper mechanism for the first strategic objective, and the commissioning of academic research into child development as the basis on which to pursue the second objective. (This case study deals only with the planning and implementation of the first objective exemplified by the introduction of the 'Lion Mark' in 1989–90).

IMPLEMENTATION

The essence of the toy safety problem was that the public had no way of distinguishing the BTHA members' products, which were developed, tested and manufactured to the world's highest standards, from counterfeits, popular lines and near-replicas made outside the control of the BTHA. These unsafe toys were usually, but not always, sold in street markets and non-traditional outlets. It was these toys, almost exclusively, which proved dangerous and attracted censure from the trading standards officers and the press.

The BTHA accepted the consultants' proposal that the solution to the problem was to give the public a means of telling at a glance which toys were safe and which were not necessarily so. A suitable

Figure 14 The Lion Mark

symbol – the Lion Mark – was designed and accepted by the BTHA Council (See Figure 14.)

The plan for the introduction of the new symbol was agreed as follows:

1. The symbol would be introduced to the manufacturing industry in sufficient time to allow packaging and moulds to be adapted to carry the Lion Mark symbol by the 1990 season.
2. The programme and the new symbol would be introduced to the authorities and safety and welfare bodies. These would include members of Parliament, trading standards officers, child welfare bodies, consumer organisations, ROSPA, toy retailers, academics, and selected media.
3. The symbol and the safety story would be launched to the general public via the media, talks to parental groups, consumer promotions and a video, 'Choosing and Using Toys'.

To ensure the success of the launch of the new Lion Mark, a wide range of facilitating and supporting activities were planned and carried out successfully:

- Training and briefing industry spokespersons.
- Publishing a regular Parliamentary BTHA Newsletter.
- Producing a range of Lion Mark merchandise.
- Operating a toy safety press bureau.
- Arranging briefing meetings for special interest groups.
- Organising a major symposium on child safety.
- Forming the National Toy Council to promote safety.
- Exhibiting at the Trading Standards Officers' annual conference.

- Exhibiting at the Department of Trade and Industry's Christmas safety roadshows.
- Liaising with retailers to train their store staff.

EVALUATION

The successful achievement of the BTHA's first objective, as described above, can be shown by the following statistics:

1. Nearly 200 toy manufacturers took out BTHA licences to use the Lion Mark. This represented 80 per cent of the UK toy sales.
2. An 'early day motion' in the House of Commons, signed by 60 MPs of all parties, congratulated the toy industry on its Lion Mark initiative.
3. The launch of the Lion Mark was covered by 43 radio and TV programmes, 19 national newspaper articles, 170 regional newspaper items, and 65 national magazine stories.
4. A dramatic decrease in ill-informed reporting in the pre-Christmas press resulted. The dramatic change in the public perception of the toy industry is illustrated in Figure 15.
5. The BTHA is now recognised by authorities at all levels as a reputable and responsible industry body. Its relations with the ITC (previously the IBA) have improved constructively, and it is invited, for example, to address the annual conference of the Trading Standard Officers on the subject of toy safety.
6. As a result of the success of the Lion Mark and subsequent customer demand, the British Association of Toy Retailers has entered into a joint initiative with the BTHA. The objective is to offer toy buying customers a way of identifying shops where safety and quality can be assured. This will be achieved by Approved Lion Mark Retailers featuring the Lion Mark within their shops.

The total budget of the scheme during the three years, including all fees, was approximately £230,000.

CASE DISCUSSION

Some of the best ideas in public relations practice are comparatively simple and straightforward. The idea of a mark of quality is not new and there have been many similar schemes launched successfully.

In this particular case, probably the most difficult problem was

Figure 15 The dramatic change in the public perception of the toy
industry after the introduction of the Lion Mark

getting unanimity within the BTHA for the funding of this
ambitious scheme. Briefing the consultants gave them *carte blanche*
to plan the implementation of the new Lion Mark.

The idea of introducing a mark of quality was fairly obvious, but
the manner in which the programme was carefully planned and
introduced is very impressive. Too often, a good idea is launched
without the meticulous attention to detail which differentiates a
reasonably successful scheme from a very successful one. In this

instance, the introduction of the Lion Mark, and all the supporting events which were organised, ensured that it made a substantial and continuing change in the public perception of the British toy industry.

Case 8.2 Women and business in Budapest

BACKGROUND

The 'Decade for Democracy' programme was created to affirm the importance of small business initiatives in the new free market system in Central Europe, to affirm the contribution that women continue to make to a thriving free enterprise system and to provide Hungarian women business owners and potential business owners with the encouragement, support and information they need to move forward successfully in their new economic system.

The programme facilitated the establishment of the first Hungarian Association of Entrepreneurial Women, resulted in 125 participants beginning new businesses and created good will for American corporations in Central Europe.

RESEARCH

Meetings were held with key individuals at the US Department of Commerce, US Chamber of Commerce, US Department of State/ Agency for International Development, US Department of Labor, US Small Business Administration, the Hungarian American Enterprise Fund, United Nations and the Hungarian Embassy to the United States. The programme was based on the research arising from the materials gathered from each meeting, references and books provided, as well as individual discussions.

The research raised the following question:

> As Hungary moves towards a free market economy, the challenge remains: How do you maintain social and economic stability while imposing a new economic system?

Planned reforms are causing economic hardship and social tension. Unemployment and inflation are rising, living standards have declined. The government is under pressure to demonstrate results from its new free market policies or to renew state intervention and control in order to avoid negative impact on the Hungarian people. The Hungarian government must provide new opportunities for employment and must promote the establishment and growth of small businesses, primarily in the private sector, in order to create networks of suppliers and service establishments that are missing in the economy.

These goals cannot be accomplished without the inclusion of women as full partners in the new market economy. Credit, capital management and small enterprise development projects should be targeted especially for women and female heads of households because they comprise a significant proportion of producers. Support for women who want to start and manage microenterprises in their communities should be a top priority. In Hungary, there is a large 'informal' sector: women who are performing small entrepreneurial activities but who are not included in government statistics. There is a need for women's organisations that provide moral support and encouragement to women as they start or expand businesses.

Large firm investment in Central Europe is critical for the growth and survival of the new free enterprise system. However, large firms do much better in the later years of a long expansion. They do much worse in a recession or when the economy is close to a turning point on the upward side. Small business generates jobs immediately. In the US, firms with fewer than 20 employees are the largest job generators in the economy, and women-owned firms are on the increase and their failure rate is decreasing.

Women entrepreneurs are making an important and well-recognised contribution to the economy of the United States. More importantly, through their success they affirm the benefits inherent in a strong free enterprise system.

PLANNING

The Decade for Democracy programme focused on women in the workforce and women business owners. In practice, these two groups overlap and there is value in including women who have not yet made a move to business ownership.

In addition to conference attendees, the National Women's Economic Alliance Foundation (NWEA) received over 200 requests from Hungarian women wishing to attend the programme. It was not possible to accommodate all these in October. Conference participants included successful American and Hungarian business owners, women in government and women in industry.

Media coverage, print and broadcast, underscored the significance of American women in the workforce coming to Hungary to provide counselling and post-conference assistance to Hungarian women.

EXECUTION

In October 1990, the NWEA, in conjunction with the Foundation for Small Enterprise Economic Development (SEED), a Budapest based organisation created to foster small business development in Hungary, hosted the first programme for women in the workforce in Hungary. The two-day forum, comprising plenary sessions and workshops, was attended by over 250 women. Approximately 75 per cent of all attendees were from Budapest with the remainder from towns and villages outside the city. This latter group had been identified and invited to attend by SEED. US corporate sponsors of the Decade for Democracy included Avon Products, American Brands, American Express and Xerox Corporation.

The joint programme between the NWEA and SEED has continued successfully. A second conference was held in Budapest in July 1991 and a smaller event in Budapest in March 1992. This was structured differently — with more workshops, as experience showed that Hungarian women prefer to work in groups rather than by speaking or asking individual questions in a large meeting.

The latest development has been the establishment of a Mentor Council which provides a forum for United States women to support the activities of SEED. A meeting of the Mentor Council was held in Budapest in September 1992. The original concept of this programme was that it was aimed exclusively at women, but in the light of experience it was decided to open the conferences and meetings also to men.

EVALUATION

In attempting to assess the results of this initiative, it is important to remember that the Hungarians have lived for many years under a regime that punished initiative, labelled entrepreneurs as outlaws of society, discouraged goalsetting as determined by the individual and tried to eradicate risk-taking and achievement.

The Decade for Democracy programme, which led to the formation of SEED, has provided real life examples of business women in the United States helping Hungarian women to face the new circumstances in their country. The meetings have shown that seeking free enterprise goals and community benefits and the quest of Hungarian women for a better economic standard of living does not threaten deeply held values.

On the practical level, it has been emphasised that it is possible to identify the process which enables volunteer networks to be created to serve as a resource for women entrepreneurs and career women as well. To this end, the NWEA worked with SEED to organise the first Hungarian Association of Entrepreneurial Women.

CASE DISCUSSION

The National Women's Economic Alliance Foundation is a non-profit organisation of women and men leaders who work together to increase career and economic opportunity for women within the free enterprise system.

The Alliance serves as a resource of concern to senior level women in the workforce. It is based in Washington DC and has associates in the US, the Netherlands, Ireland and Switzerland. The current president is Patricia S Harrison, a Washington public relations consultant, and she has taken a leading part in the establishment of the Decade for Democracy and its extension to Hungary. The power of public relations to modify attitudes can be used to promote good causes. Many practitioners work in the charitable and fund-raising fields, where they use their professional abilities to good effect. Other public relations practitioners and business executives use their leisure time to work for causes in which they believe. This case study describes the excellent work being done by groups of United States professional women to encourage women in Hungary and other countries to claim their rightful place in the business world.

Case 8.3 EUROPAMÅLET – a protest through pleasure

BACKGROUND

Sweden has one of the highest standards of living in the world. There is only one catch: it also has the highest taxes in the world. When the Swedish Government recently raised VAT on hotels and restaurants by almost 12 per cent to a staggering 25 per cent, the business community was aghast.

The Swedish Hotel and Restaurant Association (SHR), representing one of the most adversely affected groups, decided that it was time to register a protest in the strongest possible terms and to focus public attention on the likely effects of Sweden's destructive sales tax, which would be particularly hard on tourists who compare the Swedish price for meals and hotel rooms with other European countries.

KREAB, one of Sweden's leading public relations consultancies and lobbying specialists, was retained to develop and implement a campaign to protest and try to reverse this untenable situation.

RESEARCH

The main problem was that increased costs deriving from the imposition of excessive sales and employers' taxes undermine tourism and make hotels and restaurants mainly the preserve of the privileged few. Sweden has a record of consensus politics so it was agreed that strikes, boycotts and similar protests might prove counter-productive. Who loved air traffic controllers?

The agreed strategy was to adopt a policy that would evoke the sympathy of the general public. Numerous approaches were proposed and rejected, including the idea of a European standard menu. This was rejected as it would exclude non-European restaurants. The eventual solution was to select a day, advertise it nationally and offer Swedish restaurant patrons the normal menu at European prices.

A theme was needed and this was agreed as 'EUROPAMÅLET' – a Swedish pun meaning both 'European meal' and 'European target'.

Statistical data was compiled to highlight the detrimental effect of discrepancies between Swedish and European taxes and tariffs. This data included restaurant costs for purchasing food (10–25 per cent higher in Sweden); wine, beer and spirits (25–50 per cent higher); labour costs (25 per cent higher); and VAT on restaurant meals (more than 100 per cent higher). Relative rates of taxation on spirits, wine and beer were also compared with a European average tax on spirits (Sweden 92 per cent, Europe 55 per cent), wine (Sweden 59 per cent, Europe 30 per cent), and beer (Sweden 50 per cent, Europe 31 per cent).

Additional statistical data included an analysis of restaurant and hotel costs, to highlight the fact that employers' tax, VAT and labour costs alone account for more than 60 per cent of total operating costs. Projections predicting 4 to 5 per cent annual growth for international tourism, making it a leading business sector by the year 2000, were compared against Sweden's expected tourist deficit.

PLANNING

There were two target audiences: the Swedish Government and the Swedish voters. The agreed objective was to mobilise public opinion (voters) against destructive taxation, and thereby persuade the Swedish Government to revise its current policy on sales taxation and tariffs on alcoholic beverages and restaurant food.

The strategy was 'protest through pleasure'. A 50 per cent discount was offered on a restaurant meal to recruit support for EUROPAMÅLET, and to give the public a taste of European living, lower costs, improved night life and a better business climate.

IMPLEMENTATION

Saturday, 6 October 1990 was selected as the day on which about 800 Swedish restaurants were to serve EUROPAMÅLET. The campaign focused around a specially designed EUROPAMÅLET logotype which combined three elements: plate, knife and fork (see Figure 16.)

- **Phase 1**
  20,000 stickers and posters – promoting 6 October as the day of action – were printed for display on restaurant doors and windows.

Figure 16 EUROPAMÅLET logo

- **Phase 2**
  Information was distributed to restaurateurs and hotels, including large posters and place mats. The requirements were:
  — a standard menu;
  — to be open all day;
  — at least two choices of main course;
  — an adequate selection of alcoholic and non-alcoholic beverages to be served during a period of not less than four hours.

- **Phase 3**
  A mini-brochure explaining the background and aims of EUROPAMÅLET was produced and 500,000 copies distributed to all participating restaurants for issue to all guests on 5 October.

  There was also a simultaneous distribution of guidelines for local and regional advertising. Six press conferences were staged at strategic locations on 1 October.

EVALUATION

Subsequent to the implementation of EUROPAMÅLET on 6 October, a brochure was prepared confirming the success of the campaign and citing statistical results and media and public response. This was distributed widely to participants, opinion leaders, journalists and other community leaders.

- EUROPAMÅLET attracted three times the number of guests normally served on an ordinary Saturday.
- Media coverage was exceptional in Sweden's leading newspapers and the regional and local press.
- Results from an independent survey confirmed that 90 per cent of Swedes were aware of the EUROPAMÅLET campaign. Of these, 99 per cent approved of the idea and 65 per cent were aware that the campaign was intended primarily as a positive protest against the oppressive taxation imposed on Swedish restaurants and hotels.
- The brochure included an introductory letter from SHR's chairman, Nils-Erik Brundell, stressing the importance of a sound market economy, free competition on equal international terms, the removal of complex Swedish regulations and excessive taxation and the economic damage caused by apathetic politicians.

TAILPIECE

The fight continued. The Swedish Hotel and Restaurant Association continues its lobbying to persuade the Swedish Government of the strategic significance of restaurant and hotel prices in generating vital revenues from tourism and the need for intelligent government incentives.

France has reduced VAT on hotel services from 18.5 per cent to 5.5 per cent and has seen the economy boom. As part of a general package of economic incentives designed to double tourism in five years, Ireland reduced VAT for hotels and restaurants from 23 to 10 per cent, while simultaneously improving the means and cost of travel to the country. Sweden was the only country going in the opposite direction.

In Spring 1992, the Swedish Government decided to reduce VAT on food from 25 per cent to 18 per cent.

CASE DISCUSSION

This is a fairly straightforward example of an industry protesting against unfair rules and legislation which restricts its legitimate business prospects and using public relations communication methods to promote its case.

Research into comparative situations in other countries provided facts and figures which were used effectively in the preparation of the argument presented on behalf of the Swedish Hotel and Restaurant Association. The adoption of an appropriate theme EUROPAMÅLET, and a striking memorable logo, helped to focus public attention on the campaign and to win its support. The decision to select an appropriate day, 6 October, to highlight the situation brought the implications of the problem and its harmful effect on the Swedish tourist industry to the attention of the whole country.

The public relations programme was based on sound research, aided by an effective theme and logo, and pursued energetically with the enthusiastic support of the whole industry and secured the success it deserved.

Case 8.4 Promoting vocational qualifications

BACKGROUND

The National Council for Vocational Qualifications (NCVQ) was set up by the UK Government in 1986 to promote, develop, implement and monitor a comprehensive system of vocational qualifications in England, Wales and Northern Ireland. (Scotland has a slightly different and separately administered system.)

NCVQ does not award qualifications but accredits vocational qualifications (NVQs) offered by other established bodies which are often particular to an occupation sector. Accreditation follows a lengthy procedure to ensure that written standards as well as NCVQ criteria are met. These standards are set by employers, trade unions, academics and training professionals. This means that there is widespread participation in the development of NVQs and that many are the 'property' of an industry sector.

In 1988 a National Record of Vocational Achievement (NROVA) was introduced to enable individuals to accumulate training credits leading to a full NVQ. This encourages the organisation of training as well as defining a career development programme suited to the competencies and abilities of the individual. Another development is the introduction of a database of all qualifications which have been accredited. This facility is for training providers and counsellors whose task is to advise on appropriate qualifications.

NVQs are categorised in four levels ranging from those requiring the most basic numeracy, literacy and communication skills to qualifications embracing the needs of senior technical, professional and managerial occupations. The levels will be extended in due course to embrace full professional qualifications.

RESEARCH

A series of research projects was commissioned by NCVQ in 1989 with the intention that these would guide the development of a fresh communications programme. Key findings of this research included:

1. Training specialists were generally aware of NCVQ and of NVQs but lacked specific information on progress and the timescale leading to accreditation of new NVQs.
2. NCVQ was thought to do little to help company trainers win support from their own top management for new initiatives which would encourage more individuals to train for NVQs.
3. Senior managers, including personnel specialists, were not aware of NCVQ. It was noted that there is a growing emphasis on training, with additional resources being applied, but that this benefited employers whereas qualifications such as NVQs largely benefit the individual employee.
4. In terms of image, NCVQ received sympathy for its task from those who understood what it was doing. But it was not sufficiently in touch with industry, relying too much on intermediaries in the training field. This gave it a dull and academic 'feel' which was compounded by confusing and complex communications.

The research project concluded by making a number of recommendations to guide future communications and on which to base a communications strategy. These were:

- The key audience must be decision makers in industry – both at board and line management levels. Since this audience is strongly influenced by industry and professional bodies, any communications must recognise this factor.
- Individuals should be made aware of NVQs and encouraged to demand training leading to qualifications from their employers.
- The emphasis should be to brand NVQs as a product rather than NCVQ which is, ultimately, the administrative mechanism behind the qualifications.
- Messages should be selectively tailored towards different industry sectors so as to recognise special issues or concerns.

PLANNING

From the analysis of the research, a set of specific communications objectives was established. These were:
1. to distinguish the NCVQ initiative as new and original compared with other training activity;
2. to establish the role of NCVQ in relation to awarding bodies, industry groups, training providers and trade union groups;
3. to simplify the message to each target audience and explain what their role is. In particular, present specific benefits which

will encourage commitment and participation in the future development of NCVQs;

4. to move from creating general awareness of NCVQ to promoting the products: NVQs, the NROVA and Database;
5. to increase awareness of senior and line managers in the NVQ process;
6. to ensure training specialists have the practical information they need for their sector to assist them to promote NVQs within their own organisation;
7. to work closely with awarding bodies, educators and trainers to increase uptake of NVQs by individuals; and
8. to ensure the process is understood and supported by critical supporting publics such as politicians, employers' organisations and trade unions.

Meeting these objectives would be a considerable task with such a widespread audience and so many different special interests. It was decided, therefore, to break the task down into four distinct programmes, each addressed to a particular target audience and with its own set of objectives.

1. Decision makers

Aimed at those who ultimately decide how budgets are allocated and who are concerned for the future profitability and competitiveness of their businesses.

This would:

— position NVQs as the answer to an increasing need for training and a means of overcoming scepticism regarding the standard of existing industry-based qualifications;
— encourage chief executives to recognise that they should participate in their industry's training initiatives and to invest in training resources for their own company.

The public relations programme would be largely centred on media relations and use well-known industrial leaders/decision makers as spokesmen or ambassadors to testify to the value of NVQs.

Alongside this would be the use of the same ambassadors within their peer group, such as at conferences and specially created events.

2. Pre-accreditation

This was aimed to those audiences which were currently involved in the lengthy process of obtaining accreditation from NCVQ for their particular industry's qualifications. This would include employers, unions, trade associations, trainers and institutions as well as awarding bodies concerned with setting the standards and delivery of qualifications.

This part of the campaign would:

— ensure that the principles of NVQs were understood;

— explain the timing of the accreditation process;

— encourage the sectors to claim ownership of their specialist NVQs;

— promote the use of NROVA and Database products.

For this element there would be an emphasis on press relations in sectoral trade media combined with direct communication to training professionals.

3. **Post-accreditation**

Here the target audience comprised industries where accreditation was completed and NVQs readily available. The objective would be to ensure sectors were aware of existing NVQs and of new ones as they became accredited.

To reach this group there would be a concentration on resource material for use by trainers and careers advisors who would be treated as a channel of communication. In support of this, press relations would use the professional training media to explain sector NVQs and illustrate case histories of successful examples of their uptake. Broadcast media would also be used to promote success stories. Face-to-face contact would be achieved by participation in training oriented exhibitions and conferences.

4. **Corporate**

Whilst the overall strategy is to promote NVQs as a brand, there remains a need for corporate communications in support of NCVQ as the enabling body. In particular, this would aim at opinion formers: politicians, trade union leaders, professional bodies and academics.

Messages would:

— explain the credentials of NCVQ;

— position NCVQ as *the* authority on *all* vocational training;

— demonstrate the positive achievements of NCVQ.

Activity would include media relations and events to introduce news such as the annual report. Combined with this would be specific activity to communicate selected messages effectively.

IMPLEMENTATION

The following activity was undertaken:

- **Pre- and post-accreditation**
  — support for paper presented at *Flexible Training* conference;
  — speaker support and display at *Personnel Today* workshop;
  — review of *Careers for the '90s* exhibition;
  — participation in *Human Resource Development* week, including Ministerial attendance to launch *Database*;
  — presentation of a seminar at *Education Resource* exhibition;
  — organisation of stand at *Institute of Directors* exhibition;
  — participation in *Jobs 90* exhibition;
  — analysis of further exhibition opportunities related to specific sectors;
  — writing and production of new 'consumer' leaflet;
  — production of biographical information on key NCVQ personnel;
  — joint venture efforts with awarding bodies;
  — organisation of radio interview technique training for NCVQ personnel;
  — production of sector case studies covering ten locations/industries;
  — advice and guidance to careers service counsellors;
  — joint ventures, including media relations and production of collateral material for specific sectors including: agriculture, horse care, accountancy, office administration, carers, retailing, hairdressing, computer services and armed forces;
  — special programmes for the construction and engineering industries;
  — editorial features and radio interviews;
  — programme related to people with special needs in conjunction with *Remploy*.
- **Decision makers and corporate**
  — all current literature appraised for conformity to house style and recommendations made for change where necessary;
  — revision and improvement in style of newsletter and production of new style at bi-monthly frequency;
  — involvement in production of annual report;
  — placement of feature articles;
  — production of consultation document for higher level NVQs;
  — arrangement of interviews with national press;
  — issue of regular press releases on news stories;

— organisation of delegates' reception at CBI conference;
— organisation of stand and reception at *Institute of Directors* conference;
— support for NVQ holders winning National Training Awards;
— launch of NVQ *Database* and follow-up publicity including production of marketing material;
— Parliamentary activity including lunch for MPs and peers, mailing of newsletter to relevant individuals, briefing peers for House of Lords debate, reception in House of Commons, article for *House* magazine;
— organisation of a chairman's reception for senior industrialists;
— dinner for chairmen of leading companies in key sectors;
— placement of material with producers of education and business-related radio and TV programmes.

EVALUATION

Monitoring the public relations programme concentrated on comparing the quality of press coverage for three months: April 1988, April 1989 and April 1990. The new campaign started in September 1989 so the last analysis highlighted the results of the new strategy after its first six months of operation.

The measure of quality was set against the following criteria:

● Relationship with educational and training press with a shift in emphasis towards more informed debate on NVQs.
● Relationship with the national press, especially those media able to reach opinion leaders.
● Coverage of NVQ news in business journals and the trade press relevant to NVQ sectors combined with coverage of case studies illustrating NVQ successes.
● Range and quality of coverage in the regional press and broadcast media.

In total, some 2200 documents were analysed and, qualitatively, a major shift in the quality of press comment was discerned. In more recent articles, the greater emphasis on NVQs rather than NCVQ is also noticeable.

CASE DISCUSSION

This ambitious scheme to introduce a standard system of vocational qualifications was obviously going to require considerable publicity and explanation if the idea was to make any progress. This was recognised by the group preparing the programme and an in-depth research study was implemented before the action plan was adopted. The research led to eight recommendations but the caveat was issued that it would not be easy to communicate with such a widespread audience. It was therefore proposed to divide the plan into four publics: decision makers, pre-accreditation, post-accreditation and the corporate field. Each of these publics would be tackled separately.

The programme is unlikely to be completed quickly as it requires the conversion of professional bodies and companies to the new concept of vocational qualification. The active programme introduced has, however, made excellent progress as shown by the excellent media coverage which the idea has received.

A programme of this nature, which intends to change attitudes of both employers and employees is an obvious candidate for a comprehensive public relations campaign and it is encouraging that the British Government realised this instead of embarking on a large advertising campaign.

Case 8.5 Helping small businesses

BACKGROUND

British high street banks faced a great deal of criticism during 1991, mainly about their role in relation to business, and particularly to their attitude towards their three million small business customers. This controversy culminated in a request from the Chancellor of the Exchequer that the major clearing banks issue a code of practice covering their dealings with small businesses.

Barclays Bank was keen to go one stage further than its competitors and to take positive steps to demonstrate the bank's understanding of its small business customers, particularly since its major competitor, the National Westminster Bank plc had historically assumed the 'high ground' on issues concerning the small business and especially the 'start up' business.

RESEARCH

Careful research was undertaken prior to planning and launching the new programme. Arising from this research, the following public relations objectives were adopted:

1. to help to position Barclays Bank as the number one bank of choice for small and start up businesses;
2. to win a larger share of attention, particularly in the media, for Barclay's activities in the small business sector;
3. to stimulate an increased number of enquiries from potential start-up businesses about Barclay's services to this sector;
4. to raise the visibility of Barclays with certain key start-up groups, including women and ethnic businesses.

PLANNING

As a result of the pre-campaign research carried out by the London based public relations consultancy, Paragon Communications plc, the recommended strategy was as follows:

- The first step would be to produce a major report on start-up businesses, designed to provide basic facts and figures and to create a significant publicity platform for the bank. In addition to providing new insights into the market, the report would act as an authoritative work of reference, not only for the media but also for third party organisations working with small businesses.
- The production of the report would emphasise the bank's desire to understand better the start-up market in order to be able to best serve its needs.
- Specially commissioned research would be undertaken among small business start-ups, focusing on their motivations and aspirations, to provide valid new information that would be of interest to the media – including several segments important to Barclay's business – and of value to potential start-ups.
- When it became available, the report would be launched to the media and to small business organisations to create a Barclays-branded debate about the character and motivation of men and women 'who were going it alone' in business.

Prior to commissioning the research, Paragon agreed a series of key messages which the report was designed to deliver and on which its success would be judged. These four key messages would be:

1. Barclays is the number one bank for 'start ups' and small businesses.
2. Barclays understands the needs of the self-employed and small business owners.
3. Barclays provides practical support to small business customers and offers a wide range of services to help them plan and operate more effectively.
4. Barclays can act as a signpost to other forms of advice and guidance that small business customers are likely to require.

IMPLEMENTATION

The production of the report involved a number of research projects to produce the necessary information on which the final report would be based.

Independent research was commissioned among the start-up market and the general public in order to find out the personal qualities they believed were necessary to successfully set up a business. In addition, the agency commissioned two 'family group' discussions to assess the impact starting a business has on family life. The research was developed in order that the report could examine a series of themes relating to starting a business:

- The facts of life about being in business on your own.
- The views of the general public on starting a business.
- The good and adverse effects starting a business may have on family life.
- How women adapt to business.
- Special problems of ethnic businesses.
- Where to seek and obtain good advice.
- How starting a business in the 1990s compared with similar efforts in the 1980s.

Each section of the report was planned to focus on a different aspect of starting up, to enable the messages to be delivered accurately to media targeting the different key groups.

To complement the research, Paragon sourced and prepared 25 case histories, each illustrating a different aspect of starting up, to be used in the report. The case histories provided live examples of start-up businesses to stimulate media interest. The report also included individual viewpoints from organisations working with small businesses in order to present an authoritative overview of the issues affecting small businesses.

Pre-launch discussions were held with all key national, regional, vertical trade and live media in order to assess individual journalists' requirements prior to the launch date of the report. Embargoed press packs were then issued in order to give the media time to digest the information prior to the launch date and prepare story lines.

Detailed questions and answers for Barclays representatives were prepared and rehearsed so that they would be in a position to answer not only questions arising from the report but also to deal with any controversial issues which might be raised about banking practices.

Paragon arranged a formal press conference to present the results of the research. A number of the case history subjects were invited to be present at the press conference so that they could be interviewed by the journalists. Finally, following the launch of the report, a complimentary copy was mailed to all industry organisations and governmental ministers concerned with the small business community.

EVALUATION

In the six months following its launch, the 'Starting Up' report achieved over 56 million media opportunities to see three out of the four key objectives.

Results achieved included 28 live media interviews in the two days following the launch. The launch of the report did not attract any adverse publicity, despite the critical climate in which it was launched. The interest following the launch of the report was so great that Paragon and Barclays mailed out over 3000 copies of the report in response to requests from small businesses and other organisations.

Barclays' initiative has been warmly welcomed by the government minister responsible for small businesses and has done much to improve relations between the bank and the small business community in Britain.

CASE DISCUSSION

The high street banks have adopted very positive public relations programmes to improve their relationships with existing private and business customers. Codes of practice have been adopted, customers are sent letters promising personal attention and a banking ombudsman was appointed. These public relations initiatives are commendable, but unfortunately the relationship between customers and their banks has sunk to a very low level. This disenchantment has been fuelled by a considerable number of well-publicised examples of mistakes by banks and their disinclination to correct obvious errors. The banking ombudsman has reported that he received more than 10,000 complaints in the year to September 1992, an increase of 60 per cent on the previous year.

Lord Alexander of Weedon, chairman of National Westminster Bank plc, put up a strong defence of his bank's treatment of small firms when he gave evidence to the Commons Treasury Committee on 2 December 1992. Lord Alexander claimed that branch managers tried to nurse companies through a deep recession and that it was not in the bank's interest for firms to fail.

One can appreciate the need for banks to charge for services rendered, especially to non-customers, but an enhanced sensitivity and a sense of proportion would do much to redress the depths of disenchantment into which the leading banks are sinking. Many of the misunderstandings are quite trivial and a good public relations policy for the banks would be to adopt the old-fashioned concept that 'the customer is always right'. The latest news report is that a high street bank (not Barclays) demanded a fee of £3 from an old age pensioner to change a £10 note. This action was defended by the bank in question as it is in line with the bank's policy towards non-customers.

In the face of this current climate of opinion about the banks, it was courageous of Barclays to launch a new programme to secure an increased slice of the small business market sector. It is relevant to mention that many of the complaints about banks come from small business owners who have been charged large fees because of small unauthorised overdrafts, thus increasing the overdrafts substantially.

To revert to this case study, it is noteworthy that Paragon appreciated the vital part that research could play in achieving the targeted objectives. The production of the exhaustive report was selected as the main element of the programme and steps were taken to see that appropriate independent research was undertaken to ensure that the report would be a valuable contribution to the facts and figures and potentialities of the small business field. The very satisfactory level of media coverage achieved would not have been possible if the report had not been so well researched and presented.

Case 8.6 New Fish on the Block — a fishy story

BACKGROUND

The Sea Fish Industry Authority in the United Kingdom was worried by the fact that by the end of 1990, quota restrictions on the availability of the UK's favourite fish — cod and haddock — were leading to price increases. Sea Fish — the body responsible for generic marketing of fish in the UK — needed therefore to encourage consumers to experiment with new, unfamiliar species in order to prevent the frequency of fish consumption being affected.

Previous public relations programmes carried out for the Sea Fish Industry Authority by London based Paragon Communications plc, in 1989 and 1990, had focused attention on the health benefits of all types of fish, as well as the ease and convenience of preparation — messages that needed to be maintained in future programmes.

RESEARCH

Before preparing a programme of action, Paragon identified several issues which would be central to the effectiveness of the new programme. These were:

1. The support of fishmongers and fish merchants would be vital. There would be no point in encouraging consumers to experiment with lesser known fish varieties if they were not readily available for purchase.
2. The campaign had to be synchronised with the appropriate fishing season and the availability of the species.
3. The health benefits of eating fish had been widely covered by the UK national media and interest in this subject was waning.
4. Regional media would be important as a vehicle through which fishmongers could promote themselves locally.
5. The campaign needed to be flexible enough to accommodate availability and individual tastes in fish.

In order to understand fully prevailing attitudes of both fish-mongers and consumers to the lesser known species of fish and to provide information which would help to plan the campaign, Paragon commissioned quantitative and qualitative research through a leading UK research company, Taylor Nelson Food and Drink.

The results of this research were encouraging. It was clear that housewives would be willing to experiment with lesser known species if they were given advice and encouragement. Conversely, fish-mongers did not promote lesser species because they believed that housewives would not be receptive.

PLANNING

The results of this research gave valuable leads to the way in which the campaign should be devised in order to break this vicious circle. Paragon designed a programme focused on four main themes:

1. Fishmongers would be encouraged to display prominently at least two of the 'new fish' — ling, huss, coley and whiting — between 30 September and 12 October. To secure their cooperation, they would be provided, free of charge, with eye-catching point-of-sale material, together with full details of the consumer support activity.
2. The dissemination of health messages would be continued.
3. Opportunities would be created for a spokesman role for fishmongers and Sea Fish home economists.
4. Efforts would be made to generate substantial editorial publicity.

IMPLEMENTATION

The following activities were undertaken:

1. Campaign identity. Four caricatures of the 'New Fish on the Block' (see Figure 17) were created to appear on all printed campaign material. The characters — MC Huss, Lin-da-Ling, Kev Coley and Sharon Whiting — were designed to be warm, humorous, appealing and media friendly, attributes not usually associated with cold, wet fish.
2. Trade briefings for representatives of the major UK retailers and their wholesale suppliers. Elements of the campaign timing were amended in the light of their comments.
3. Fishmongers were made aware of the campaign through their trade media and by a direct mailing which included an opt-out mechanism. All retailers and merchants were regularly updated with information about the progress of the scheme.

Figure 17 'New Fish on the Block'

4. Women's consumer press were kept fully informed. Briefing/tasting sessions were held in the Sea Fish Kitchen for journalists from the top UK circulation weeklies and monthlies, using recipes incorporating nine different fish species. Press kits were distributed to attendees and non-attendees.

5. Point of sale material was produced for use by all participating fishmongers, including recipe leaflets, collectible sets of badges, 'empty-belly' posters for highlighting species available and window display tickets. Complete packs were mailed to all participants approximately two weeks prior to the start of the campaign.

6. 'Press Ad', a division of the UK Newspaper Society, was used to distribute material to all regional and local newspapers for use in advertisement features immediately prior to and during the two weeks of the campaign. This provided fishmongers with an opportunity to promote themselves through their local media.

7. A nationwide regional media tour was organised, involving three Sea Fish home economists and local participating fishmongers. Full briefing notes and campaign messages were supplied and recipe leaflets offered in 48 pre-negotiated interviews.

8. National and regional media activity included teaser information supplied to the broadcast media early in the campaign with follow-up material three weeks prior to launch. Press kits were distributed to all national and regional newspapers immediately prior to the launch. Opportunistic tactics included the delivery of a whiting with a press release to BBC Radio 1 and London based Capital Radio which both resulted in on-air mentions. A story was developed with the national tabloid *Daily Star* on fish tests with schoolchildren.

EVALUATION

The 'New Fish on the Block' campaign secured massive coverage in all sectors of the consumer media. Highlights included TV-AM, the *food and drink* programme on BBC 2 TV, the *Jimmy Young Show* on BBC Radio 2, national dailies, mass circulation women's magazines and 48 regional radio stations. The quality of media coverage was high, with an average of two of the three agreed consumer messages being delivered in each item. These consumer messages were:

- Shoppers should be more adventurous in their choice of fish, experimenting with new, less familiar species.
- New, less familiar species offer excellent quality, delicious taste, are value for money and are easy to prepare.
- There is a wide variety of fish available at your fishmongers.

Only 20 out of 2200 fishmongers opted out of the scheme and the feedback from participating retailers was excellent.

In a random sample of 40 fishmongers questioned after the campaign, 38 said that it had been a very good exercise and 35 were willing to take part in similar activities in the future. Sea Fish estimated that sales of at least three of the four lesser known species features increased significantly during the period of the promotion.

CASE DISCUSSION

This case study won a trophy in the 'Marketing new product' category of the IPRA Golden World Awards for Excellence and is an excellent example of public relations being used effectively and imaginatively in a marketing context.

It might be said that media attention can be secured easily for anything to do with food but to achieve such useful and widespread exposure in the media requires considerable creativity and experience of how the media operate. This case study shows how research was used successfully to establish the main objectives and the campaign was planned very carefully to make the best use of cooperation from the fishmongers who supported the scheme.

The use of caricatures lent a focus to the programme and undoubtedly helped to make the general public aware of the special promotion of these types of fishes with unfamiliar names. It would be interesting to know to what extent the demand for these new species of fish persisted after the promotion ceased.

Case 8.7 Opportunist public relations – 'Eggwatch'

BACKGROUND

Public relations representatives and counsellors usually feel most productive when they are able to create and implement programmes which are strategically based and appropriately targeted.

Long-range planning usually makes for the most effective programmes. However, we occasionally have an unexpected situation arise which allows us to take advantage of a sudden opportunity, ie, to take a 'problem' and make it a public relations 'opportunity'. That is exactly what happened with the 'Billboard Birds' programme created for Dean Foods, a leading dairy and food processor in the United States, which is based in suburban Chicago.

Dean Foods is a highly respected company, originally family-owned and renowned in the midwestern and southern United States. The dairy has a reputation for being a good neighbour – both in local communities where its products are sold, and in the dairy and food industries. Dean Foods is a client of Cramer-Krasselt, America's fourth oldest agency, which offers integrated marketing communications services, including advertising, public relations and direct marketing.

In the spring of 1991, an outdoor advertising campaign had been completed for Dean Foods. The campaign included colourful billboard signs showing milk being poured into a glass with the line, 'Dean's ... bursting with freshness'. Part of Dean's milk container was shown, including its famous little bluebird logo. The sign had been displayed on many billboards, but when workers scaled scaffolding to change one particular sign located on the highway between Chicago and Milwaukee, Wisconsin, they were dive-bombed by a beautiful, gigantic hawk. The creature had a four-foot wing span, formidable curved talons and a chestnut-red tail. The male hawk had built a nest on the back of the billboard, where his mate was preparing to hatch a new family! Who could have predicted that a sign for a dairy would turn into an aviary?

After doing some research, Dean Foods executives and the sign company learned that the birds were protected under the Migratory Bird Treaty Act (a federal law), and could not be disturbed. The sign would have to stay up until the baby hawks were hatched, which would take approximately one month. As a result, Dean would receive an extra month of visibility free of charge.

RESEARCH

When Cramer-Krasselt began working with Dean Foods, the agency conducted qualitative research which led to a key insight: consumers of dairy products do not easily differentiate those products based on attributes. Consumers of dairy products base their buying choices more on the personality of the product and the company. Another important consideration is that the target audience is women, and especially mothers with young families. That target audience implies a broader audience: children/families.

As stated above, Dean Foods has an excellent reputation due to a variety of benevolent activities and sponsorships throughout its history, mainly because it was originally owned by a family who valued being a good neighbour. Fortunately, their family philosophy was also an excellent corporate position, especially for a company which sells a family-oriented product. Getting involved with the US Fish and Wildlife Service in the protection of a young family of hawks ideally fitted into Dean Foods' corporate value system and philosophy.

Cramer-Krasselt therefore interviewed representatives of the US Fish and Wildlife Service. Although the service had never received a corporate donation before, it had no policy against it. There was never enough operating monies from the subsidies received, and the service was very open to the idea of receiving a donation.

PLANNING

Dean Foods was already on the right side of the issue: they would do nothing to disturb the nest. In fact, they would do everything possible to protect it.

As a result of a creative session in the agency, Cramer-Krasselt recommended that Dean donate the month's rental fee they would have normally been charged to the US Fish and Wildlife Service, and wrap a publicity programme around the unusual circumstances and the donation. Dean agreed to donate $1500 to the service, and an additional $500 to help launch a Milwaukee-area hawk research foundation. They were most enthusiastic about helping the family of magnificent hawks. But they were also excited about publicising the modern urban folktale; after all, the strange location for a nest could provide plenty of mystery — and plenty of whimsy, considering the bird on the company's logo!

In the intensely competitive dairy industry, institutional image is crucial. Dairies operate regionally and depend heavily on high levels of local awareness. In creating an institutional programme built around the nesting hawks, the objectives were:

- to generate goodwill and enhance Dean's public identity within Milwaukee through media interest;
- to extend the story's interest to Chicago media;
- to take the opportunity to help wildlife;
- to underscore Dean's reputation for being a good neighbour;
- to add top-spin to the advertising.

CREATIVITY

While creativity is the icing on the cake in most public relations activities, in this case, it was the cake itself. Even though it was home to a family from a protected species, a nest on a billboard could possibly be considered to be of marginal news value, unless some endearing and charming elements were added.

The agency ascertained the creative elements which would be essential to the programme's success:

- naming the programme;
- a special piece of creative writing, be it a poem or verse;
- creation of a picture opportunity near the sign, and thereby, the hawk eggs/chicks.

The programme was dubbed the 'Eggwatch' programme, and a poem entitled *The Ballad of the Billboard Birds* was written. The agency also created a special cheque presentation ceremony near the sign. A Dean representative and an official from the US Fish and Wildlife Service were on hand for the ceremony. The ballad follows.

IMPLEMENTATION

The agency immediately planned a press conference for the cheque presentation ceremony.

Using the new name of the programme, special news release stationery was created with a bold *Eggwatch News* graphic spanning the top of the page. The letterhead underscored the sentiment of

THE BALLAD OF THE BILLBOARD BIRDS

Now here's our tail of hawks out browsing
For the ultimate choice in hi-rise housing.

One day they spotted the perfect decor
Along Interstate 43-94:

A billboard ad for milk from Dean's,
A lovely place for birds of means.

And since their kids should have the best,
These red-tailed hawks settled down to nest.

The only thing is, a brand new sign
Is s'posed to go up about this time.

But these protected birds are proud
And human beings aren't allowed.

So the sign stays up until the day
The little ones can fly away.
(repeat verse)

Of course, the folks all speculate
About this strange place to locate.

Who'd have thought an ad for a dairy
Would turn into an aviary?

It's either the milk the red-tails savor,
Or the company's logo's a real good neighbour!

the situation and posed the possibility that the birds were attracted to the sign by the bird on the company logo.

The Ballad of the Billboard Birds was reprinted in the press materials. By turning an odd situation into a public relations opportunity, additional spin-off opportunities arose. The programme was developing in progress. The publicity which resulted from the cheque presentation ceremony was very positive: Dean Foods agreed to the production of video 'b-roll' (an American term for raw video news footage which can be edited and used by television news departments), and an additional press conference when the eggs were hatched. The b-roll was sent with press releases and reprints of the ballad to television news assignment editors at cable and network affiliated stations in nine priority states. Dean also agreed to production of a music score and setting of the poem, *The Ballad of the Billboard Birds*.

Building on the idea of a modern urban folktale, a local folk music group composed the music and recorded the ballad. They also recorded an instrumental version, in case on-air talent would want to sing along. The agency quickly sent out songsheets with tapes and press releases to local and national radio journalists.

After issuing a news coverage memo heralding the hatching of the chicks, another unexpected and nearly tragic situation arose. The new mother hawk was hit by a car on the Saturday before Mother's Day (an American holiday honouring mothers) as she was foraging for food for her young. Dean immediately made additional monies available for a local wildlife specialist to nurse the mother hawk back to health, and at the same time help the father continue to feed the chicks. (The female hawk is responsible for tearing up the food the male hawk brings back to the nest.) A donation was made to *Critter Control*, the local environmental wildlife group which provided the specialist who aided the mother and family.

Once again, a press conference was called on site. By now, the red-tailed hawk family had become 'media darlings' of sorts, with reporters following-up the story consistently. Instead of having to call the media for placement, the public relations people were receiving media calls for further information.

At all three press conferences, pictures were taken to increase the base of the publicity placement efforts. As stated at the beginning of this chapter, Dean Foods was renowned for being a good neighbour both in local markets as well as in the dairy industry. Therefore, photos and press releases were serviced to dairy industry publications. Additionally, bird magazines and periodicals were sent materials.

EVALUATION

Of course, evaluation must go beyond mere quantity. In the Dean Foods Billboard Birds case, quantity was achieved: the total audience reach was 24,924,730. But it is important to consider the quality of the news coverage, and then weigh the quality and quantity against the total cost of the programme:

- The quality of the news coverage was excellent. Both Milwaukee and Chicago television and newspapers provided extensive, sympathetic coverage. Dean Foods was positioned as the hero.
- Significant and prestigious national news coverage was achieved via a report placed with the highly respected American broadcast journalist, Charles Osgood, who is on CBS-RADIO and TV. Mr Osgood not only played the ballad music and read the verse on 'The Osgood File' (his regular morning national radio report), but also created his own verse to go with the instrumental version of the music. In that report, he even tipped his hat to the public relations people for doing a good job and providing a good public service. The three-minute report was aired four times during the peak morning rush hour. There were seven Dean mentions in each report.
- Positive coverage also appeared in food and dairy trade magazines. The agriculture industry was reached via placement on 'Ag Day', the nation's largest agricultural news television programme. Editors of the programme aired the b-roll. Additional television stations in the states of Illinois, Wisconsin, Iowa, Indiana and Tennessee (Dean target markets) and even *Bird Talk Magazine* covered the story.

In virtually all coverage, Dean's was prominently and positively mentioned. A large number of media used the company logo connection (the little bird), especially gratifying on television.

The project generated goodwill as well. Reporter Kay Dawes of the *Chicago Sun-Times*, said she received 'many nice calls' from readers about her photo feature (photos supplied by Dean's).

US Fish and Wildlife Service was tremendously appreciative in a letter that said: 'Because of [the birds'] site selection and media coverage, we can bring environmental education, especially as it relates to raptors, to the public.'

All of this was achieved for the nominal sum of $7000.

In the end, however, an evaluation of any consultancy's programme is based upon the client's perception, and the feedback he or she receives. In this case, Dean Foods received praise from its industry and target audience. This praise meant as much as, if not more than, all the news coverage.

CASE DISCUSSION

In a capitalistic society, there is much emphasis on marketing and/ or acquiring and keeping a good public image. Often, public relations professionals must corral resources and energies to promote the sales of products and/or the company's good deeds. Of course, such activities usually lead to increased business and, thereby, success for all those involved. But what is particularly rewarding is when public relations professionals not only have the opportunity to garner favourable publicity for a profit-making concern, but also achieve something for the greater good in that process.

Sometimes that extra 'something' merely involves being aware of what kind of situations are occurring around us and our businesses, and how we can turn those situations into opportunities. In the case of the Billboard Birds, the public relations people learned of a situation which they saw as an opportunity. While strategic development is always the most important element of programme planning (and really drives the creativity), creativity itself is a key element in opportunistic public relations. Creation of copy and graphics should complement the subject matter. That doesn't mean that a serious subject cannot be communicated with a little humour also. It does mean, for example, that when the product is used by mothers for their children, the communication and activities can be whimsical, fun and entertaining, as well as for the greater good.

In this case, highly creative elements were married to a benevolent activity arising from an opportunity. The result was goodwill and excellent news coverage for a company, and most importantly, the healthy growth and development of three little members of a protected species.

Case 8.8 Potatoes from Idaho

BACKGROUND

The Idaho Potato Commission asked Creamer Dickson Basford, a US public relations consultancy, to organise a one-day event which would affirm the branded identity of Idaho potatoes with consumers and would correct the widespread erroneous idea that Idaho is a generic name for potatoes grown in the United States. It was also hoped that organising such an event would help to correct the reluctance of the media to mention Idaho potatoes by name.

RESEARCH

In order to investigate fully the various aspects of the situation before proceeding to plan the event, the consultants looked at the possibilities from four vantage points – consumers, media, advertising and sales.

Consumers have a high awareness of Idaho potatoes. Surveys revealed, however, that while consumers prefer Idaho potatoes, a majority believe mistakenly that they are a generic variety that can be grown in other states and are unable to distinguish them from other russets. With little help from signage at supermarkets, consumers had limited resources at point-of-sale to help them shop for Idaho potatoes. Additionally, consumption data indicated that potatoes were losing ground to rice and pasta.

While media analysis indicated that target consumers chose network and broadcast TV news, drive-time radio and were heavy readers of 'vertical' print – business, science, health, travel and food, media coverage was limited to food section recipes using Idaho potatoes as an ingredient. Surveys revealed that media could not distinguish and saw no merit in specifying the Idaho brand. Advertising compared the quality of Idaho potatoes to the superior Idaho growing environment but was limited to 30-second spots on television and half-page spreads in women's magazines. Sales of Idaho potatoes got off to a slow start at the autumn harvest time and did not peak until the winter holidays.

The conclusion reached from the research was that the challenge was 'no small potatoes'. It was necessary:

1. to find a way to get the media to convey the exclusivity and superiority of Idaho potatoes;
2. to show consumers how to shop for and buy genuine Idaho potatoes;
3. to demonstrate that Idaho potatoes could be fun, nutritious and contemporary; and above all
4. to get the message to consumers via broadcast news and vertical print and thus stimulate demand earlier in the year, at harvest time.

PLANNING

The target public was broadly defined as women aged 25 to 44, middle income and with children. The media was also a key audience. The obvious short-term objectives were:

*   to break down the barrier of editorial resistance to brand mention;
*   to begin to build awareness about the exclusivity and superiority of Idaho potatoes and to determine how this could form the basis of future programming.

The immediate measurable objectives were agreed as the following:

1. to generate targeted media coverage quite separate from food page recipes, in vertical print and on broadcast outlets;
2. to convey the superiority of Idaho potatoes;
3. to stimulate sales at the start of the traditionally slow season;
4. to portray a contemporary, fun image for Idaho potatoes.

These preliminary considerations led to the adoption of the main strategy which was recommended: to organise a special harvest event. This would have four supporting strategies:

1. to create immediate, widespread media impact with stories appropriate to major national news and vertical media outlets;
2. to focus attention on the superiority of Idaho potatoes;
3. to secure publicity and media attention at the start of the season;
4. to take a very light-hearted approach to the whole campaign.

IMPLEMENTATION

To emphasise the association between Idaho and potatoes, it was essential that the planned event be held in the state. A harvest festival had been held for 62 years in the small, remote town of Shelley, Idaho, the heart of the potato producing region. However, it no longer excited local reporters and the nearest major media bureau was a two-hour plane journey away. While the festival lasted five days, the main events were on the Saturday, a time when media resources are particularly scarce. Furthermore, all media resources were focused at the time on the Iraqi Gulf situation.

The problem was how to get a high level of media coverage of an unknown event in a tiny remote town. The solution which was adopted was to rely heavily on humour. A pun-filled, three-part teaser campaign was developed, using a postcard of an oversized 'spud', a limited edition poster depicting Marilyn Monroe clad in an Idaho potato sack, and a children's Grand Tuber legend. This 'SPUDtacular' story was supplemented by highly targeted story angles carefully constructed to appeal to vertical media with key messages central to each report. Some of these key messages included a branded marketing challenge of a seemingly generic product, the effect of the weather, ideal growing conditions, science improving on a super spud, health, better quality and better nutrients.

Throughout the teaser campaign, targeted pitch letters and intensive telephone follow-up, the agency succeeded in attracting the attention of distant national broadcast television bureaux who were convinced by constant contact to call their local affiliates and set up coverage. As one (formerly sceptical) local reporter said, 'It's no big deal around here, but it sure seems to be a big story nationally'.

Exclusive pre-event interviews were scheduled on syndicated and regional radio programmes and also interviews on television on the day of the event. Appropriate spokespeople that were recruited included a University of Idaho scientist, speaking on science, weather and the environment; the Governor on economy, business and the ideal environment; the executive director of the Idaho Potato Commission on the marketing challenge; local farmers talking about the environment, crop quality and state standards; and Idaho chefs discussing culinary appeal.

To ensure plenty of fun, variety and continuing news appeal, special activities and displays were organised. These included an attempt at the Guinness record for potato peeling; a ceremonial first dig of the season's crop by the Governor; exhibits featuring unusual uses for potatoes, from hand cream to ice cream, and a culinary exhibition featuring Idaho potato specialities.

Press materials were designed and produced that reflected the simple, rustic nature of the Idaho potato. All targeted national magazines and metropolitan daily newspapers received comprehensive press kits with press releases on the harvest events as well as the supporting story angles. Selected media received their press kits in a burlap Idaho potato sack stuffed with a one pound sack of Idaho potatoes and such Idaho-seal-bearing potato paraphernalia as an Idaho potato microwave cookbook, a potato peeler, a potato slicer, a refrigerator magnet and a T-shirt.

To supplement on-site media coverage, the agency produced and disseminated an 'Idaho Potato Party' newsfeed via satellite to the major commercial and broadcast networks. Over 100 stations across the country also received a 'Why Idaho?' video news release explaining the role of Idaho's environment in providing a superior potato exclusive to the region.

EVALUATION

By all criteria for media coverage, messages and sales, the SPUDtacular event was a success.

The Idaho Commission was very well satisfied. The sales season got off to a spectacular start with shipments of potatoes up nine per cent in the slower months of September and October compared with the same months in the previous year.

The analysis of the media coverage makes impressive reading. The event:

- attracted media features far beyond recipes on the food pages, with major coverage on national television, syndicated radio (six outlets feeding over 2000 stations) and in vertical outlets;
- delivered specific messages about the exclusivity and superiority of Idaho potatoes;
- stimulated increased sales;
- showed how Idahoans enjoy potatoes in fun, off-beat and amusing ways.

Media coverage produced more than 410 million media impressions. Stories in major television news outlets included five separate live, on-site airings by weatherman Spencer Christian, including one five-minute spot with Governor Andrus on ABC's 'Good Morning America'; half-hourly broadcasts all day on CNN's 'Newsday' and

'Headline News'. Also on ABC's 'World News this Morning', NBC's 'Sunday Today' and hundreds of regional and local network programmes across the country. Syndicated and regional radio broadcasts included the market challenge story on American Public Radio's business programme 'Marketplace', and a consumer affairs story on 'As it Happens', UPI Radio Network's 'Consumer Focus', USA Radio Network's 'Hourly News' and Copley Network's 'Newsflash'. Wide print coverage included AP, UPI, Mirabella's 'Travel Section', the *Washington Post*'s 'Health' section, and extensive food section coverage that went far beyond recipes.

Analysis of the messages delivered found that 100 per cent of the stories named potatoes in conjunction with Idaho. Many stories delivered the two primary messages more than once. A conservative count based on total stories revealed that 88 per cent of the stories clarified that Idaho potatoes come exclusively from Idaho and 64 per cent described the Idaho potato's superior attributes. The fun and fashionability of Idaho potatoes was evident in over half of the stories.

CASE DISCUSSION

This case study is an interesting example of what is often called 'marketing public relations'. Public relations is very often a significant part of a marketing campaign. In this particular instance, the public relations agency was the main, if not the sole, actor in the marketing programme.

It is difficult to think of a more challenging assignment than the need to publicise a particular type of potato and to stake its claim for exclusivity and superiority. The United States is a huge country and the story of Idaho potatoes would hardly have hit the headlines had it not been for the inspired decision to use humour as the main weapon. The Idaho Potato Commission was able to recruit a remarkably strong supporting cast, with Governor Andrus prepared to play an active part.

This case study, like Case 7.2 ('Using Rembrandt to promote health in Australia') needed some gimmick or bright idea to arouse widespread interest in what is intrinsically a fairly commonplace, if important subject. Having decided to use humour as the core ingredient of the campaign, Creamer Dickson Basford pulled out all the stops and achieved a remarkable success.

Thinking of the use of gimmicks in public relations, one is reminded of the campaign in the United States for the launching of a new dog food. The successful gimmick in that case was the decision to organise a state-wide campaign for the best singing dog. Gimmicks can only be used once, and with great discretion, but can transform a run-of-the-mill event into an exciting media one.

Idaho potatoes featured in the American pavilion at the 1958 World Expo at Brussels. It was reported that practically the whole of the budget was spent on the rather beautiful pavilion, leaving little for mounting a creditable display inside. As a result, one of the exhibition rooms had a large showcase in its centre featuring a huge Idaho potato with a caption extolling its virtues.

9

Art and Culture

Case 9.1 The Bamboleo story in Tampa, Florida

BACKGROUND

Political and racial considerations came unexpectedly at Tampa Bay in Florida to interfere with the annual invasion, parade and free street party which had been looked forward to eagerly by the citizens of Tampa. This annual parade was organised by Ye Mystic Krewe of Gasparilla and the 1991 event was to be special because Tampa had won the right to stage the 1991 Silver Anniversary Super Bowl. Non-Americans are unlikely to be able to appreciate the importance of the Super Bowl organised by the National Football League (NFL). There is very keen competition from all the cities in America to be asked to stage the annual event.

Tampa had staged Super Bowl No XVIII very successfully and their reward was to be invited to stage the prestigious Silver Jubilee Super Bowl in 1991. The promise of a 'stunning array of concessions and donations' and the community wide celebration and festival immediately prior to the game day had helped to clinch their success. The Super Bowl task force was jubilant and all the preparations for a wonderful occasion were proceeding smoothly until four months before the event when the 'Ye Mystic Krewe of Gasparilla' invasion and parade were cancelled.

This disaster was the result of concerted allegations of racism and sexism by a black coalition. The group demanded immediate investigation of the private, all-white 'Krewe'. The aggrieved groups promised protests and demonstrations and threatened to use the internationally televised Super Bowl game to expose their complaints to the world.

The controversy divided the local community. The National Football League expressed great concern. Twenty-one black organisations publicly demanded equal economic opportunities.

The national media discovered the controversy and thrust Tampa squarely into the national spotlight. To complicate matters, the crisis in the Middle East and protests from environmentalists and other rights groups added to the growing crisis facing the parade and festival. The environmentalists had stopped power boat racing the previous year in order to protect the manatees (sea cows) which spend winter in the warm bay area waters. They challenged whether the manatees would be safe during Gasparilla. The Gulf War started in January, just days before the Super Bowl. Fears of terrorist attacks spread. Concern mounted for spectator safety at the Super Bowl and the festival events.

These issues raised questions hard to answer:

- Does the community want the parade?
- Can the safety of Super Bowl guests and Bay area residents be assured during the parade and the street festival?
- Would there be sufficient police and security to meet possible dangers?
- Would the festival be well attended despite the terrorist threats?
- Could a top quality parade and festival be organised in less than four months?
- Where would the funding come from?
- Could the public concern about the issues which had arisen be met and their trust and understanding be restored as the planning moved forward?
- Could the parade and festival be a catalyst to provide economic opportunities for black minorities?

RESEARCH

For the last 86 years, the annual Gasparilla Pirate Invasion and Parade had been sponsored by the 'Ye Mystic Krewe of Gasparilla', an all-male, all-white private social organisation. On 6 February 1990, under perfect weather conditions, the event drew its largest crowd ever with nearly 250,000 visitors packed into the 2.5 mile route. Everything was perfect and plans for the February 1991 event and the Silver Jubilee Super Bowl were proceeding smoothly and on schedule. The NFL and Tampa's Super Bowl Task Force were very pleased.

Then literally overnight, everything changed dramatically by a seemingly unconnected event on 11 August 1990. A PGA golf tournament at the racially exclusive Shoal Creek Golf Club caused a public uproar and raised questions about the Krewe and the parade plans as women and blacks are excluded from the Krewe. Ironically, only a few days before the Shoal Creek episode, some of Tampa's most influential business and political leaders and other groups had participated in a solidarity march against prejudice and bigotry. The City of Tampa's mayor had an excellent record of eliminating discrimination in city government.

The following week, the NFL met with Tampa's Super Bowl Task Force to discuss minority participation in 'Gasparilla'. A coalition comprising 21 black organisations formed a unified front to challenge the Krewe's racial exclusion policy. They presented an eight-point economic plan calling for immediate integration in the Krewe and more minority participation in economic opportunities in the Super Bowl and other community activities, now and in future. The coalition threatened boycotts against targeted white businesses. Local and state-wide media, and even major national media like the *New York Times* reported on the critical situation and the delicate negotiations taking place in Tampa.

Discussions continued in the hope of reaching a compromise that would satisfy all parties. In September the Krewe met and rejected the demand that blacks and women be admitted. Further, they relinquished their sponsorship and all responsibility for the parade and festival. This was quite unexpected and caused shock and disappointment. The same day, the mayor announced that a new parade would be planned by the Chamber of Commerce, the Tampa Coalition (a bi-racial race relations organisation created three years earlier) and the Tampa/Hillsborough Convention and Visitors Association (THCVA). The THCVA and its executive director thereafter assumed complete responsibility for the new parade. With little more than three months left to plan, a 15-member Super Bowl Parade/Festival Steering Committee was appointed.

For several months, the issue of blacks becoming members of the Krewe remained one of the main issues. However, the central focus became the lack of economic opportunity for black minorities, not only during community events like the Super Bowl, but in general. The black coalition insisted that the black community had been excluded too long. For example, full opportunities should be made for minorities to participate in the parade, over and above the few traditional black bands that had performed in the past years.

It was necessary to separate and focus the issues. What was perception and reality? Both had to be addressed. The parade and festival committee would see what could be done to meet the need to include minority participation. The city's leadership, primarily the mayor and chamber of commerce, was addressing the minorities' economic concerns and would make significant and meaningful changes during the next few months. In the meantime, extensive research was undertaken to find out whether the community really wanted the parade and whether all the problems of ensuring a really successful festival could be overcome in the short time remaining.

The results of the research revealed an overwhelming majority in favour of the parade and festival taking place. Further, there was a consensus that the parade should be open to a broader and culturally diverse representation of Tampa's ethnic groups.

PLANNING

The decision having been taken to proceed with the festival under new management, the various sub-committees began planning the many complex and different aspects of the project.

There was little time left to create a completely new theme, name and logo for the new parade and for building up public support. Newspaper articles in the local and national press reflected the frustration of the community about the many issues surrounding the Krewe controversy. Many people doubted if a really creditable event could be planned in such a short time. This apprehension was a major obstacle the Steering Committee had to face in planning Bamboleo. Another problem was convincing sponsors that the event would take place at all and would be of a quality comparable with previous years.

Research emphasised that the new parade could not be associated, even remotely, with pirates or to anything related to Gasparilla; therefore a new name had to be developed, communicated and supported by the community. The Parade sub-committee coordinated a 'name the festival' competition. Through promotion by the local newspaper and popular radio station, the contest attract 300 entries. From these, 25 names were selected and finally five names were brought to the Steering Committee. The winning name was 'Bamboleo'. It was chosen for its thematic appeal and because it encompassed Tampa's ethnic community.

The Steering Committee and the THCVA public relations staff worked together to plan and execute all media responses, news releases, media alerts, fact sheets and media briefings. The THCVA public relations staff attended the Steering Committee meetings and their counsel was invaluable throughout the whole time the committee operated.

The public relations staff familiarised themselves with all the research results and planned all the publicity, timing and content of announcements, as well as the media briefings. They produced 15 media releases and arranged six media briefings. Through their efforts, dozens of articles were generated in the local press. They also prepared media kits for the briefings held to announce the plans for the parade route, the entertainment and sports stars participating in the parade and festival, the new parade name and the unveiling of the logo. The public relations manager also acted as backup to all the spokespeople.

New issues arose. The Ku Klux Klan (KKK) and also a veterans group supporting American POWs left in Vietnam both requested permission to march in the parade. The KKK felt the situation surrounding the Krewe was unfair and they wanted to march in protest to display white supremacy. The veterans group wanted to protest against lack of support in the United States for the POWs. The deadline for entries had passed by several weeks and so the two group's requests were refused. The KKK bought reserved seats and eight hooded and robed members watched the parade.

This new unexpected issue had a chilling effect on the plans and extra efforts were made during the weeks leading up to the parade to assure the community that the parade would not be cancelled.

EVALUATION

Parade organisers, city officials, the NFL, area residents and Super Bowl guests pronounced the Super Bowl Bamboleo Parade and Festival a huge success. Despite the cold, rainy weather, the subdued mood of the community, the absence of the Krewe and their pirate ship and potential terrorist threats, an estimated 150,000 attended the parade and another 70,000 attended the free street party festival. Almost no adverse publicity resulted from the Gasparilla controversy during Super Bowl week — compared with the wide publicity generated when the issue first surfaced.

Following Bamboleo, signs of hope emerged for a resolution of the Krewe controversy. Many residents and members of the Krewe offered congratulatory comments on the Bamboleo efforts and expressed hope that the pirates could come back in the future.

The bad weather and the more reserved mood of the attendees created a much different atmosphere for the 1991 community celebration. The police reported no arrests at the parade and only four at the night street festival. Officials reported no public drunkenness or rowdiness which had been part of Gasparilla's past. The gay rights activists, the black minority groups and the Vietnam

War handicapped veterans group all threatened to protest and demonstrate during the parade and during the internationally televised Super Bowl game. However, no protests or demonstrations were executed by the threatening groups, which is indicative of the community's attitude to the multi-ethnic efforts made by the Steering Committee.

An editorial in the *Tampa Tribune* stated: 'Party goers experienced a rare treat − a Tampa parade that sounded as great as it looked ... not everyone loves a parade, but those who do found plenty to love at Tampa's first Bamboleo'. The NFL Special Events coordinator said: 'You could have written a whole book about this one game. You had Gasparilla, a war, all the extra security, and the racial questions about the parade. But everything was terrific and went smoothly. Tampa delivers what it promises. The enthusiasm in Tampa can hardly be matched elsewhere'.

The most important success of Bamboleo was the way in which the black community had been integrated into the whole event. The chairman of the black coalition was pleased. He said 'I believe that a good effort was made, and I believe that a reasonable level of participation was achieved'.

TAILPIECE

The mayor vowed that Gasparilla would return in future years because it is one of the top ten community events in the United States. The standard of openness for the parade which was achieved by including all ethnic groups (blacks, Hispanics, whites) in the parade would continue. In 1992, Gasparilla did return but retooled to be more inclusive and more representative of Tampa's rich ethnic community.

Acknowledgement for this case study is due to Harriet Gonzalez, a Tampa public relations consultant who was an active member of the Steering Committee and chairman of the sponsorship sub-committee. The Steering Committee had overall responsibility for the whole arrangements of Bamboleo, including the very important public relations strategy.

CASE DISCUSSION

Considering this remarkable sequence of events which suddenly erupted to envelop what was originally just a repetition of a successful annual event, fills one with admiration for the civic heads and residents of the Tampa Bay area who could have been excused if they had taken the easy option of abandoning the whole project in view of all the adverse circumstances. To their credit, they faced each new issue as it surfaced and achieved their objective of staging a highly successful Bamboleo. It was a cruel irony of fate that failed to repeat the good weather conditions of the previous year but despite the rain and cold the 1991 Bamboleo was an undoubted success.

It is clear that the public relations efforts played a major part in securing media support and understanding during the vital months before the Super Bowl. The major impression, however, is of a community facing up to a sudden realisation of social and economic racial problems and seeking racial integration and harmony as a means of solving them.

Case 9.2 Santam's Child Art Project in South Africa

BACKGROUND

This scheme has been operated by the large insurance company, Santam, for 31 years. The company's name *Santam* is an acronym of the original name when it was registered in 1918 – Suid-Afrikaanse Nasionale Trust en Assuransie Maatskappy (South African National Trust and Assurance Company). The child's art project has three main branches: child art, bursaries for school leavers and bursaries for art students.

South Africa does not have one central education department. The system is fragmented into provincial education departments (Cape Province, Transvaal, Orange Free State and Natal). It is further fragmented in that 'black', 'coloured' and 'Indian' schools fall under completely separate education departments. Certain venues like halls may be only open to certain race groups – these are referred to as 'closed venues'. 'Open venues' are public places where people of all races may meet. Santam has always insisted on holding its exhibitions at 'open venues'. With the scrapping of apartheid this has changed and, in theory, all venues are now open.

RESEARCH

The company has acted in the firm belief that commerce and industry must make a positive contribution to the cultural, educational and moral welfare of the entire Southern African community. The short-term insurance industry is generally seen as 'hard' and at times even uncaring, and the company looked for a project which would show that it has a 'soft' side.

Research at various departments of education in South Africa revealed that there was no project such as child art conducted on a national basis and the concept was welcomed by senior members of the educational system. Against this background, Santam launched its first Child Art Project in 1963. The broad purpose of the original project was:

1. to encourage an appreciation of art among the young;
2. to create in the mind of the young a sense of trust in the future of South Africa;
3. to allow children of all races to share in a common project;
4. to afford the company exposure at a level other than business.

It was never a competition as such and at the request of the education authorities, children were not given cash prizes. Monetary awards are only made to the schools or in the form of bursaries for further study.

South Africa is both a First World and a Third World country with several languages and cultures. Over the years, care had to be taken that themes with a common interest should be adopted so that all children, regardless of their race, culture or language background could participate.

Research revealed that university bursaries to study art were virtually non-existent in South Africa and the awarding of bursaries to school leavers was introduced. The granting of bursaries was extended further to cater for students at universities throughout South Africa. What had started as a purely childbased project expanded to meet the demand for help for students to attend universities or *technikons* throughout South Africa. The bursaries are not limited to fine art or sculpture, but are also available to students of subjects such as clothes design, photography and graphic design. The scheme changes year by year to meet demand and there is continuing research at grassroots level through visits to schools and art centres throughout the country to talk to art teachers and encourage them to participate, and also to determine changing needs and to adjust the programme accordingly. Research is also done at provincial level with art inspectors and with senior educationists at national level.

PLANNING

Planning of the Child Art Project starts a year ahead with the selection of a theme. This is done in conjunction with the judges. Santam always tries to choose themes which are educational, leaning towards environmental consciousness and which are in tune with national or international trends. For example, the theme chosen for 1991 was 'Our Precious Earth' which was seen as a contribution to international concern for the survival of our planet.

Invitations are sent out to thousands of schools inviting them to participate. Brochures setting out the conditions are also despatched. The press, television and radio are also advised of the new theme by issuing a detailed press release.

The judges are normally art inspectors from various centres in South Africa. Suitable venues for the opening and the tour of the new exhibition are chosen and plans made for the transport of the items. Six weeks before the closing date for entries, a reminder is sent out to schools alerting them to the fact. Temporary staff are alerted to be ready to sort the 20,000 entries which are usually received each year. The entries are sorted into age groups and arrangements made to return unselected entries to the schools and art centres.

Bursaries

Students are invited to apply for bursaries and are required to submit a portfolio of their work by way of colour slides. One panel judges the work of the school leavers and another panel judges the work of the university and technikon students. The works of the bursary winners are collated for distribution to universities and technikons for viewing.

Each year a new budget is prepared and submitted to management for approval. The regular adaptations made to the project are also presented to management for approval. Almost without exception they are accepted. The budget for 1991 was R 424,500 (US$ 155,000). In recent years, real costs have always been between 1–2 per cent of budget.

IMPLEMENTATION

The project is handled in-house and falls under the jurisdiction of the public relations manager. One person, the Art Projects Coordinator, is assigned to the project and does virtually all the work except during the days when judging and selection takes place when some temporary workers are taken into service and colleagues are also required to lend a hand. The project is not advertised and no use is made of outside agencies apart from one graphic designer.

Apart from Santam's own travelling exhibition, other exhibitions are selected to meet special needs. Over the years, special educational projects have also been mounted — an art teacher's training project; a special graphic art project for schools and a full colour brochure of all the selected works.

Selection — child art

About a week is set aside for the selection of the child art works. During the 1991 project, material had to be selected for three exhibitions:

- Santam's travelling exhibition;
- an overseas exhibition;
- an exhibition for child art competitions overseas.

The judges view every entry and set aside works of merit. These are then viewed a second time (and a third time if necessary) to come down to a reasonable number for each age group and the exhibitions concerned. In 1991, of the 17,000 entries, 89 were selected for Santam's own exhibition, 33 for overseas exhibitions and 38 for overseas competitions.

When the process is completed, the designer comes in and with the judges selects the works which will be used in the company's calendar. Rejected entries are returned to the schools concerned. Telegrams, letters of thanks and congratulations are despatched. The works are mounted for exhibition.

Selection — bursaries

The bursary entries of both school leavers and university or technikon students are viewed by separate panels of judges. Their portfolios are considered but actual works themselves are not judged.

Exhibition opening

All arrangements have to be made for the formal opening of the exhibition at a function in one of the major centres. There is also the occasion for the handing over of certificates and prizes to the pupils who come to the opening function. In the other centres, the medals, certificates and cheques are presented by local Santam managers.

Touring exhibition

After its official opening, the new exhibition goes on tour for a year and is open to the public in 20 different centres. At the end of the touring period the works are suitably framed. Some are used in Santam's own offices while other permanent exhibitions are sent elsewhere, including overseas.

EVALUATION

The project is believed to be the largest national child art project in the world which is run by private enterprise. Elsewhere these projects are under government sponsorship.

The number of entries has increased from about 4000 in the early days to around 20,000 and the number of schools participating has increased three-fold – evidence of the acceptance of the scheme at grassroots level.

Excellent press coverage is enjoyed throughout the year at national level and at regional level as the exhibition tours. In 1990, 25 press releases resulted in 876 press, radio and television reports. Nearly 40,000 people each year visited the touring exhibition during recent years.

At the World Child Art Competition in Taiwan, South African child art works received far more awards than much larger countries such as the United States. There are three permanent Santam child art exhibitions in South Africa, and four overseas in the United States, Brazil, Germany and Israel.

The number of school-leavers competing for bursaries has increased from 36 in 1988 to 94 in 1991. As far as student bursaries are concerned, the number of entries increased from 100 in 1988 (the first year) to 150 in 1989 and 236 in 1990.

Follow-up evaluation has shown that the original objective was surpassed in that participation in the scheme could well have been the incentive to direct certain people into creative careers.

Each year, about 35,000 child art calendars are printed and distributed in South Africa and abroad to people or institutions which have requested them. Branches request and distribute the calendars to business connections while members of the public are also entitled to collect calendars.

TAILPIECE

Case studies of the history of winners in the scheme also form part of the evaluation although strictly speaking they fall beyond the scope of the objectives. Several of those who participated in the Child Art Project over the years have gone on to full-time art-related careers. A good example is the story of Tommy Motswai, a deaf-mute who was one of Santam's first bursary winners in 1985. He has gone on to make a distinguished art career. He is only one of many men and women who won awards in the Santam projects and have gone on to make their mark in art and related professions.

In a territory with so many different races and languages, art can play a useful harmonising role. There are two official languages in South Africa – English and Afrikaans. Apart from the many European and Asian languages spoken at home, there are no fewer than 23 'black' languages falling into four main groups.

This case study is handicapped by the impossibility of including here some of the fine colour paintings which have won acclaim in the Santam Child Art Project. Figure 16, however, shows examples of the high standards which this project has encouraged for 30 years. Figure 17 shows some of the numerous press stories.

CASE DISCUSSION

This is a remarkable account of a nationwide public relations programme carried out successfully for 30 years despite the constraints of apartheid and other political restrictions.

An insurance company relies on its reputation to support its marketing activities. In 1963, the company realised the importance of its corporate image – the public's perception of the organisation. Its belief in corporate social responsibility was encapsulated in its statement that large organisations in commerce and industry must make a positive contribution to the cultural, educational and moral activity of the whole community.

One must admire Santam's persistence in developing and expanding this imaginative public relations programme in the face of many problems. The way in which this scheme was introduced and expanded to meet popular demand is a classic example of a large service company using public relations to provide a valuable service to the nation's children and young people. It is interesting to note that there was no advertising support used and this decision was justified by the ample support received from the educational authorities and the schools in response to direct approach. A project of this nature must rely heavily on public support and the case study shows that this was forthcoming in ample measure.

The project had many favourable characteristics:

- It provided a service to the nation's children and young people.
- It appealed to all racial groups.
- It was a scheme that could look to the well organised educational sector for support.
- Each year attracted new entrants and sustained national and regional interest, so it was a project which would not date.

Figure 18 Drawings from the Santam Child Art Project

Figure 19 Santam's Child Art Project – press reports

- The scheme could be relied upon to secure continued media attention. Apart from the main story, the programme is bound to provide an almost endless supply of human stories as youngsters succeeded in their entries.

Art effortlessly crosses frontiers and cultural and racial divides. Santam should be commended for adopting such a community friendly scheme and carrying it out so successfully and consistently.

Case 9.3 The Asakusa Picture Scrolls in Tokyo

BACKGROUND

The Bunka Shutter Company of Tokyo manufactures a wide range of building and housing materials, including shutters, doors and partitions. The company was established in 1951 and enjoys a high reputation in the Japanese construction industry.

Shops need heavy shutters for security before and after business opening hours but these shutters are usually very drab and devoid of any visual attraction. The Bunka Shutter Co Ltd, in conjunction with the Dentsu PR Center Ltd, devised a scheme for making shop shutters visually pleasing and adding to the attraction of the locality.

The objectives of the scheme were threefold:

1. to improve the attraction of shutters;
2. to provide a framework for depicting the art and culture of the local community;
3. to be capable of publicising communal anniversary events and announcing local activities.

The rationale for this ambitious scheme was the desire to see the Asakusa district regain its former eminence which had become eroded by the attractions of the newer districts of Ginza, Shibuya and Shinjuku in the western sectors of Tokyo.

PLANNING

Asakusa was chosen as the site of the project. This area is well known at home and abroad as a tourist centre boasting such attractions as the imposing Kaminarimon Gate and the shops along Nakamise Street.

As one of the objectives was to promote the art and culture of the local community, motifs appropriate to the area and the Nakamise shopping district were selected. The scenes depicted on the scrolls illustrate features of the district reflected in the traditions of the common profile through festivals, markets, customs and habits retained from the Edo era.

Art and Culture

Tokyo National University of Fine Arts and Music also cooperated in the project to raise the artistic and cultural value of the shutter painting visuals. The university is located in Ueno, near Asakusa, and its participation helped to accomplish the revitalisation and cultural promotion of the district.

Two anniversary events of the local community afforded an excellent opportunity to pursue the ideals of the scheme. The Nakamise shops association celebrated its centennial and 1988 witnessed the 30th anniversary of the reconstruction of the main building of Sensoji Temple.

The scheme went ahead smoothly through a three-way relationship between the local shopkeepers' association, the shutter company and the university. It was the combined efforts of these three bodies that ensured the speedy success of the project.

IMPLEMENTATION

The actual Asakusa Picture Scrolls project was made up of the following items:

1. Location and scale. The shutters are about 2.3 metres high and up to about 360 metres along the Nakamise shopping street. Four scrolls depict the traditional culture of Tokyo's Asakusa district.
2. The theme of each scroll depicts Asakusa's seasonal events and characteristic sights enjoying long traditions. The themes shown on the scrolls were:
   — The *Sanja Festival*. This is one of Tokyo's major festivals. Sanja is a harbinger of summer.
   — *Hozuki* (Chinese ground-cherry) Fair, a summer event featuring market booths lined up in the grounds of the Sensoji Temple.
   — *Ukiyoe* – genre paintings expressing the life of the common people in the Edo era.
   — *Dances of a golden dragon and a white heron* – elegant dances handed down at the Sensoji Temple.
3. The actual production and supervision of the scrolls was executed by 16 members of the teaching staff of the National University of Fine Arts and Music. Professor Sawato Fukui headed the group which was supervised by Professor Ikuo Hirayama, world famous for his 'silk road' painting series. He is now president of the university. Each of the four scrolls averages about 10 metres long and is painted in Japanese style

with delicate colour tones appropriate for expressing the traditional Edo period culture.

4. Bunka Shutter Company was responsible for putting the final design of the pictures onto the shutters. This was achieved by applying the pictures to the shutters with a new 'Marking Film' method. After the delicate colour tones of the Japanese paintings were analysed into 64 different colours, the pictures were magnified 10 times and copied onto 80 micron vinyl chloride sheets, which were then attached to the shutters.

5. The whole project took over a year to complete and as the various stages of the work were reached, the media were kept fully informed of developments. The response of the print and broadcast media was continual and enthusiastic and finally very congratulatory when the completion of the Asakusa Scrolls was announced.

6. Since the pictures appear on the shutters, they can only be seen after the shops close at 8 pm. Moreover, all the scrolls cannot be seen from any one vantage point because they are 360 metres long. To make up for these inconveniences, a number of commemorative souvenirs were produced. These included an Asakusa Picture Scrolls Calendar, picture postcards of a selection of the scrolls and framed pictures.

EVALUATION

The main objective was to revitalise and popularise the area. This was achieved without doubt by this imaginative scheme. Japanese as well as foreign tourists have flooded the area to view the scrolls, despite the late hours. The shutters have triggered a new sightseeing boom that is leading to a more extensive revitalisation of the whole Asakusa district.

The cultural influence of the shutters has also been noteworthy. Professor Hirayama has remarked: 'The street itself has become an art gallery. Utilising space in this way is epoch making. I am very happy to have been able to take part in this project'.

The media summed up the project thus: 'A fantastic environment has been created. This should serve as a guide for the cultural city of Tokyo in the new age'.

The Asakusa Picture Scrolls project was awarded a special prize by the Japanese Society of Commercial Space Designers in the 1989 Commercial Environment Design Grand Prix.

CASE DISCUSSION

This is a remarkable example of a very imaginative idea carried out successfully with the help of many different groups who had to be enthused sufficiently to win their support. This case study could equally appropriately have been classified under the 'Community Relations' section of this book, as the successful completion of the project has undoubtedly made a massive contribution to the welfare of the local community.

The contrast between a street of closed shops with drab shuttering, compared with the same street ablaze with colour and artistic beauty is breathtaking and is a concept that Japan can be proud of. Its nearest comparison is probably the fairly new custom of British contractors to use the boards round major construction sites to apologise for any inconvenience caused and sometimes to incorporate a modest amount of advertising. The building of special windows in the screening to allow passers by to watch the work in progress is another public relations device which has considerable merit. These simple but effective ways to seek favour with the people passing a site, pale into insignificance compared with this remarkable initiative of bringing an art gallery into the streets. It would not have been possible without the remarkable technical achievement of reproducing the delicate colour tones of the paintings onto thin vinyl sheets.

Case 9.4 The Third Vienna Opera Ball in Istanbul

BACKGROUND

Istanbul is a very sophisticated and cosmopolitan city, with many well-established luxury hotels, so any hotel promotion needs to be imaginative and unusual to capture the attention of the public.

This report describes the successful combination of the management initiative of the swissôtel 'The Bosphorus' and the professional advice and expertise of IMAGE Public Relations Limited.

The swissôtel 'The Bosphorus' is located in Istanbul, Turkey and is part of the multinational swissôtel hotel group headquartered in Zurich. The hotel is one of only two Turkish 'Leading Hotels of the World' so its image and reputation is already established. However, increasing competition from the other Istanbul luxury hotels demands a creative and imaginative approach to reinforcing the hotel's positioning and promoting it as the first choice for discerning influential clients.

In 1992, senior swissôtel management in Istanbul, having secured a contract to hold the world-renowned Vienna Opera Ball at the hotel, asked IMAGE for their advice and cooperation in the promotion of the ball. The swissôtel has now hosted the event for three years and this report describes the 1994 ball.

The specific objective of the programme was to reinforce the prestigious nature of the hotel, reflected in an event synonymous with elegance, charm and grandeur – all of which symbolise the essence of the swissôtel and the public it wishes to attract. In addition, the event is a huge fund-raising project for the Gurson Children's Health Foundation.

RESEARCH

In order to ensure the success of the programme, it was necessary to research thoroughly the background of the Vienna Opera Ball so that the event in Istanbul should be the same unforgettable combination of music and drama celebrated in Austria since 1877, and furthermore, to establish why such an event should be of any relevance in modern-day Turkey.

For Turkish high society, the Vienna Opera Ball has become a reminder of an almost forgotten tradition. Therein is a golden opportunity – the revival of a dearly-held custom, a history waiting to be tapped and a return to the glory years. The management of the swissôtel recognised the importance of such an event and the potential positive goodwill that can be derived from holding the Vienna Opera Ball in Istanbul.

PLANNING

Objectives

The first step was to discuss with the hotel the objectives of the public relations programme. These were agreed as:

To recreate the Vienna Opera Ball at the swissôtel 'The Bosphorus' in order:

1. to reinforce the hotel's prestigious image as the first-choice hotel in Istanbul for the discerning client, by means of an annual event which reflects the elegant essence of the hotel;
2. to raise money for charity, endorsing swissôtel's philanthropic role within the Turkish community.
3. to reach existing and new publics, including: (i) the youth who will be the hotel's clientele in the future by giving them and their parents a night of nostalgia which will always be associated with swissôtel; and (ii) a community rarely targeted – the German-speaking Turkish contingent of VIPs and their associates;
4. to establish the event, at home and abroad, under the guise of the Vienna Opera Ball, as the only débutantes' ball in Turkey and the event at which young people are introduced to society;
5. to gain sponsorship from multinationals for funding and networking;
6. to reach international markets attracted by exclusive weekend packages.

The planning process commenced in April 1994 and the ball's successful implementation demanded regular and very close liaison between the hotel and the public relations agency. Operational action plans were drawn up and regularly updated. There was a unanimous desire to improve upon the experience of the two previous events.

The plan included contractual agreements with performers, arrangement of sponsorship, distribution of promotional literature and liaison with the media. There was discussion on the best way to convert the ballroom into an 'opera house'.

It was decided that, unlike all other Vienna Opera Balls held outside Austria, the guests at swissôtel 'The Bosphorus' should dine in rooms outside the ballroom, thus keeping faith with the original format.

Profiting from previous experience, it was decided to alter the order of events. This improvement was achieved by guests dining before rather than after the demonstration polanaise. This ensured that guests were not kept waiting for their dinner and contributed to a better flow of events without any disruption from the catering.

Measurable critera

The impact of the event can be measured by the following:

1. the number of ticket sales, funds raised and sponsorship;
2. room occupancy of the hotel;
3. the media coverage and public response.

Target publics

The publics which it was desired to reach were identified as:

- current and potential hotel guests;
- the higher strata of Turkish society;
- students and alumni from the English/German/French-speaking schools in Istanbul;
- senior business people and multinational representatives;
- the media;
- the international markets.

The strategy

The strategy of the programme was to achieve the following:

1. an increase in attendance at the Vienna Opera Ball at the hotel compared with previous years;
2. financial support and sponsorship;
3. wide media coverage;
4. increased future use of the hotel bedrooms and other facilities.

IMPLEMENTATION

The promotional literature and the advertising conjured up a picture of a night to remember for the *créme de la créme* of Istanbul society at the Vienna Opera House. The promise was to provide an experience of traditional charm and magic of an evening enhanced by the entire Wiener Opernball Orchestra, accompanied by a tenor and soprano, the Schrammer Orchestra and the swissôtel Philharmonic Orchestra and demonstration dances performed by Turkish débutantes and members of the Wiener Ballet Company.

The media used

All media channels were used to promote the event – radio, television and selected press – to ensure the awareness of all targeted publics, both at home and overseas.

Promotional literature and press releases were distributed to all media channels, a press conference was held at swissôtel, and selected television stations were invited to film the actual event. Posters, mailshot letters and invitations were sent to all targeted publics and the better local schools received advance invitations for students to receive dancing tuition from an Austrian teacher who would choose the best 64 couples to perform the opening polonaise.

Interest was heightened by the recreation of a theatre box in a local high-class shopping centre and another in the hotel foyer from which promotional literature was distributed and which played a video of the Vienna Opera Ball in the two preceding years. The hotel also constructed a giant open-air lighting display advertising the event.

The hotel reached breakeven point, but the management's intention was that the ball should be a successful public relations programme and fund-raising event rather than a profit-making exercise. So 200 out of the 1200 tickets available (at a cost of $150 each) were donated by the hotel to the Gurson Children's Health Foundation for direct sale to their patrons, thus raising $30,000 for charity.

Liaison with management

The whole project was undertaken on the initiative of the swissôtel general manager so everything had the full support of management. Regular liaison and communication with hotel personnel at all levels ensured their total commitment to the event.

EVALUATION

The public relations programme for the Vienna Opera Ball, begun in April 1994, was carried out as planned and in accordance with the agreed timetable.

The media coverage was excellent and targeted at the appropriate audiences. Satisfactory sponsorship was received from major multinationals. Ticket sales and revenue far exceeded former years: 1200 guests attended and the money raised for charity was approximately $30,000.

Attendance of the children of local dignitaries was much increased, thus reinforcing the event as the accepted introduction to adult Turkish society. The hotel filled 89 per cent of its accommodation capacity.

The ball was regarded by the hotel management, the guests and the media as an outstanding success, and the best to date. The hotel thus achieved its major objective of enhancing its prestigious image and ensuring interest in the event in future years and, though unquantifiable, of selling the hotel, its services and facilities to a wider public.

IMAGE provided the senior management with a bound report, detailing the planning, implementation, media coverage and feedback of the 1994 Vienna Opera Ball in Istanbul.

CASE DISCUSSION

It is very difficult to think of new events which will captivate the imagination of the public and attract wide support. The Vienna Opera has a wonderful aura which is well known to opera lovers and the general public. The holding of the ball in Istanbul thus starts with a positive advantage but it is necessary to capitalise on this by careful planning and meticulous attention to detail.

It is interesting to note how Betul Mardin and her team at IMAGE, jointly with the hotel team headed by general manager Edouard Speck, wove together three different concepts — a débutantes' ball, a glittering musical and gourmet occasion and a fund-raising appeal for a favourite charity. Sometimes the attempt to achieve several different objectives detracts from the overall success. This report shows, however, how careful and imaginative planning can achieve many disparate objectives.

There is often a danger of an event beginning to lose its attraction through familiarity but this is not likely to occur in this instance as there will always be new débutantes and it is likely that the Vienna Opera Ball in Istanbul will be even more successful in future years, provided new ideas can be grafted on to its present successful pattern.

10

International Public Relations

Case 10.1 A Vision through the Tunnel

BACKGROUND

The decision to link England and France by the Channel Tunnel opened up many commercial opportunities for the regions at both ends of the new link. Pas de Calais, a *département* of north-west France, quickly recognised the need for improving awareness of the region if it were to have any hope of attracting inward investment.

The Communication Group plc, a London-based public relations consultancy, is a major shareholder in the Entente International Communicational SA group consisting of leading independent consultancies in the UK, France, Germany, Belgium, the Netherlands, Spain, Italy and Austria. The Conseil Général (elected departmental council) of the Pas de Calais decided to commission a media relations programme in the UK, France, Germany and the Netherlands. Each section of this campaign was to be autonomous and the UK element would be the responsibility of The Communication Group under its managing director, Peter Hamilton, with Emma Brierley as the account director.

The brief was to concentrate mainly on the business press and the whole international assignment was to be completed within six months.

RESEARCH

Before the programme commenced, the image of Pas de Calais in the UK was evaluated in depth. Fifteen one-to-one telephone interviews were carried out with targeted journalists representing a broad range of publications, including national newspapers and the trade press. All the journalists were asked about their knowledge of

Pas de Calais and for their opinion about the *département*. The findings highlighted the lack of any detailed knowledge of the area but with the imminent opening of the Channel Tunnel interest in the region was increasing.

The results of the initial research indicated that the first step must be to educate and enthuse journalists about Pas de Calais, encouraging them to write about the region and the new opportunities offered by the opening of the Channel Tunnel.

Additionally, a databank of information on Pas de Calais was established which included details of the *département's* economy, geography, demography, infrastructure, culture and leisure facilities. This databank was kept continually updated and easily accessible, providing invaluable support to activities at all stages of the campaign.

PLANNING

Following a meeting with the client in France at which the results of the survey of the UK journalists was communicated and strategy discussed, the objectives of the media relations campaign were agreed as follows:

To attract UK investment, both multinational and small business, by:

1. creating a strong identity for Pas de Calais;
2. raising awareness of the benefits for British business in relocating to Pas de Calais.

As little had been published in the UK press previously about Pas de Calais, the success of the media campaign would be measured by the level of the media coverage generated.

The media list

It was decided to target a wide range of the UK media including:

- national press;
- trade press:
  — business
  — transport
  — property
  — high tech
  — tourism

— industrial/manufacturing;
● local press — especially in Kent.

The message

Using the results from the qualitative research conducted with the journalists, it was decided that the key messages to be communicated would be:

1. Pas de Calais is strategically located at the gateway to France and at the heart of a potential market of over 100 million consumers.
2. Pas de Calais is near to the UK, home to the French end of the Channel Tunnel and offers British business a pan-European state-of-the-art transport infrastructure.
3. Pas de Calais is a cost-effective location for UK business in terms of property prices and business incentives.
4. Pas de Calais has a young and highly educated population.
5. Pas de Calais offers a high quality of life in terms of leisure and cultural facilities.

The media relations campaign would include development of a press pack, distribution of news releases, a press trip to Pas de Calais, and identification of a suitable event in the UK which could be used to promote the Pas de Calais region.

The budget for the UK media relations campaign for Pas de Calais was US$34,500 in fees and US$3700 for expenses.

Regular contact was maintained with the client through monthly reports on all activities and a monthly press book of media coverage.

The staff in the consultancy developed a good working relationship with the head of communications at the Conseil Général, offering not simply a translation service of the client's own work for UK journalists, but advising on the different approaches to be taken with British journalists as compared with French ones. Unsolicited assistance on the copy for the UK advertising campaign was generally appreciated and the consultancy became a sounding board for a number of initiatives which were not strictly within the public relations remit.

EXECUTION

The time constraints meant that a wide range of activities had to be planned and executed in an unusually short period of time.

The first decision was to create and adopt a slogan: 'Pas de Calais – a Vision through the Tunnel', which could be used throughout the campaign as a unifying factor.

The official opening of the Channel Tunnel would obviously provide a focus to generate interest and excitement in the British press about economic and political conditions on the other side and this event became the cornerstone of the media relations programme.

In order to maximise coverage on Pas de Calais, the press pack was mailed approximately ten days before the date of the Tunnel opening and direct contact was made with those journalists identified as covering the opening.

The press pack

Careful attention was given to making the press pack as comprehensive as possible. It included separate fact sheets on different aspects of Pas de Calais,

- **Key facts and figures**
  Concise, easy-to-read lists of basic information relating to the location, infrastructure, geography and economy of the area gave an informative introduction to the subject.
- **Business facts**
  An overview of the businesses operating in the region, the current level of foreign investment and the range of services and incentives offered to companies interested in relocating to the region highlighted possibilities for British involvement.
- **Industry**
  The main industries in Pas de Calais were spotlighted as transport, tourism, food/food processing and plastics.
- **General information**
  Facts and figures stressed the exceptional lifestyle and quality of life available in Pas de Calais.

The press pack, which was contained in a colourful folder with the Pas de Calais emblem, was mailed to all target media together with a news release announcing the launch of the Pas de Calais promotion and marketing campaign in the UK.

Follow-up media liaison

The initial distribution of the comprehensive press pack was followed up by regular distribution of news releases on key aspects of the area including:

- the likely impact on Pas de Calais of freight services beginning to go through the Channel Tunnel;
- the decision of Haagen Daas to centre their operations in Pas de Calais.

Two-day press visit

On the principle that 'seeing is believing', a highly successful two-day press visit was organised to highlight the potential benefits for British business of relocating in Pas de Calais.

Carefully selected national and trade publications were invited and the party included the business editor of *The Observer*, the industry correspondent of *The Times*, the European editor of *Estates Times*, the business correspondent of *Enterprise Magazine* and the editor of *Transport Magazine*. This was an excellent response for an extended overseas visit.

A balanced itinerary was organised including visits to foreign companies which had relocated in Pas de Calais. Discussions were held with local chambers of commerce and local development agencies, visits to cultural and tourism sites were organised as was a tour of key economic centres (Boulogne and Calais), and there was ample sampling of the local cuisine.

Operational difficulties identified

One problem was the difficulty of obtaining media coverage which focused on the whole of Pas de Calais and not only on the major economic and cultural centres of Calais and Boulogne, which are already well known in the UK.

The individual towns within Pas de Calais had different messages and problems and therefore it was difficult to ensure that the region promoted itself in a coordinated and disciplined manner.

EVALUATION

There is an abundance of published articles, features and news items to show that this international campaign succeeded in raising awareness of the proximity of Pas de Calais to the Channel Tunnel – and thus to the UK – and the attractions which the region offers to British industry and commerce.

The journalists who had been interviewed at the beginning of the campaign on their views of Pas de Calais were contacted again to assess if their level of knowledge of the region had increased.

Without fail, the 15 journalists all knew much more about Pas de Calais than at the beginning of the media relations programme and were interested in being kept informed of further developments in the area. The initial objectives of educating and enthusing the media had thus been achieved.

The comprehensive press pack generated numerous enquiries from a wide circle of journalists requesting further information for articles and features and the press pack became the foundation for all activity.

The wide publicity about the opening of the Channel Tunnel was used to create interest in Pas de Calais and it was possible to establish the *département* as the spokesperson on the implications of the new tunnel link for both French and British business. It joined Eurotunnel as another recognised source of reliable information for the UK media.

Numerous interviews were arranged and a number of special features resulted, including:

- Channel 4 News – UK family relocating in Calais;
- *The Times* – (i) Northern France has much more to offer than beer-stacked hypermarkets; (ii) French exploit opportunities; (iii) Channel Tunnel revives the vision of chance to compete;
- *Guardian* – Calais sees gold at the Tunnel end;
- *Observer* – French woo UK firms;
- *Sunday Telegraph* – implications of the Tunnel on Pas de Calais;
- *Transport Magazine* – stealing a march on the British;
- BBC programme 'Good Morning Anne and Nick' – advantageous property prices in rural France.
- *Chat* magazine – weekend breaks in Pas de Calais;
- *Kent Messenger* – a number of detailed reports.

The journalists who participated in the two-day press visit have written in-depth features on the potential of Pas de Calais for British business.

The results of the media relations campaign were presented formally to the client who appeared to be well satisfied. Discussions are proceeding for the possible extension of the campaign during 1995.

CASE DISCUSSION

This case study supports the accepted theory that in international public relations it is possible to plan globally but action must be local. The success achieved in a short time frame and within a comparatively small overall budget would not have been possible without the existing comprehensive familiarity of The Communication Group with the UK media. This facilitated the selection of the appropriate British media and individual journalists to be targeted and avoided any language difficulties.

This is a good example of a network, based in different countries, working together simultaneously but independently for a major client.

This case study is, of course, a report on a particular set of circumstances but the methods employed are typical of those appropriate to securing good media coverage for a foreign client.

It is noteworthy that special care was taken by The Communication Group to maintain frequent and regular contact with a senior representative of the client, for lack of this close liaison is a frequent cause of friction and dissatisfaction.

Case 10.2 Wir Stimmen für Europa (We vote for Europe)

BACKGROUND

The joint campaign of Austrian industry 'Wir stimmen für Europa' (We vote for Europe) was set up by the Federation of Austrian Industrialists and the industry section of the Austrian Chamber of Commerce. It was one of several Austrian public relations campaigns aiming at the common goal of securing a majority vote for saying 'yes to Europe' for membership of the European Union (EU) at the referendum on 12 June 1994.

The Federation of Austrian Industrialists is an organisation representing industrial interests, based on the voluntary membership of about 2000 Austrian companies. The Austrian Chamber of Commerce is based on the compulsory membership of all Austrian entrepreneurs.

The campaign 'We vote for Europe' was run throughout all nine regions of Austria during a limited period of only ten weeks. The very short duration of the campaign was due to the late decision on the date of the referendum, which was only decided in March 1994.

RESEARCH

An opinion poll was carried out throughout Austria in December 1993 by the Austrian Gallup Institute with a sample of 2000. A poll about the image of industry included ten questions about the attitude to, and expectations from, the consequences of EU membership. At that time, 48 per cent of the Austrian population were in favour of membership, 40 per cent were against and 12 per cent said they had no opinion on the subject. Other opinion polls nearer the date of the referendum showed a continuous fluctuation and the percentage of undecided persons reached over 20 per cent.

PLANNING

Objectives

The campaign's priority was first to address all the persons in the undecided group, and to convince them of the desirability of voting 'yes'. The target was to achieve a distinct positive result at the referendum. Throughout all the campaign, efforts were made to secure an open dialogue and to exchange clear explanatory information.

Target publics

Austrian industry, having as its motto: 'Partner Industrie' (Partners of Industry), decided to stick primarily to its traditional target group, ie industrial employees and their families, a group amounting to approximately one-fifth of the Austrian population.

A secondary target group of 200,000 was to be found in services related to industry.

The group of entrepreneurs and employers, as well as their representatives nominated as 'EU delegates', represented another priority group but they were already convinced of the importance of Austria's EU membership, so they could act as multipliers of the message.

Budget

The total budget allocated to the campaign was US$9 million.

IMPLEMENTATION

The campaign was designed to be confined to public relations activities and not to use advertising.

A federal 'Mr Europe' for Austria was appointed to represent the campaign in public, as well as several representatives in the federal regions of Austria. About 600 member companies appointed 'EU delegates' to act as multipliers of information within their companies. These 'EU delegates' attended regular regional meetings where they were briefed and also had an opportunity to exchange information.

A colour folder was produced and 10,000 copies were distributed to member companies of the two organisations. The folder listed and explained all the information material available to the companies and included an order form for requesting further information.

The information material produced varied from elaborate brochures to simple, concise leaflets which explained the advantages and disadvantages of Austrian membership of the European Union. Other available material included a video, posters, stickers, buttons, flags and self-adhesive stickers for company cars. A special EU edition of the board game Trivial Pursuit – 'Eurotest' – proved very popular.

Articles on various aspects of the EU were submitted for use in company magazines and newsletters.

A speakers' service was established for company events, providing companies with knowledgeable speakers who could give information and discuss with the employees the pros and cons of EU membership.

A special EU hot line was set up in the Department for European Integration and International Economic Relations of the Federation of Austrian Industrialists.

Special roadshows

Two different roadshows were designed for outdoor and indoor events and were made available to member companies. These roadshows provided a suggested programme to offer a platform for discussion and information among company employees. They were adapted to suit individual companies' needs and included information, a quiz, a touch-screen monitor and various give-aways.

A colour employee magazine *Der gute Tip* was issued four times to member companies and the last issue before the actual referendum reached a circulation of 500,000 copies.

Initiativen für Europa (Initiatives for Europe)

'Initiativen für Europa' was a separate activity, conducted under a different logo and title. It had an office, organising and coordinating citizens' action committees in all federal regions with the support of the federal and regional 'Mr Europe'. An advertisement in the major daily newspapers invited all Austrians to become active in the campaign for Europe. A launch event was organised where several well-known Austrian personalities explained why they were in favour of Austria joining the EU. This 'Initiativen für Europa' activity attracted 3000 EU activists to support the campaign.

EVALUATION

The response to the information campaign was encouraging. Approximately 1250 companies participated, so the campaign message reached about 65 per cent of all industrial employees.

The total number of items supplied was quite substantial. It included 500,000 brochures, 140,000 buttons, 100,000 car labels, 25,000 'Eurotest' versions of 'Trivial Pursuit' games, 17,000 posters, over 5000 flags in different sizes and 1700 videos. The information displays were set up 150 times and 64 companies made use of the roadshows.

The overwhelming majority referendum vote of 66.4 per cent for entering the EU was quite conclusive. The credit for this success was claimed by many organisations. A poll carried out the day after the referendum showed that 27 per cent of the Austrian population considered the different campaigns had been a major source of their information. However, 25 per cent stated that discussing the subject at work and the information they received there had influenced their decision to vote 'yes'. This was quite a positive confirmation of the success of the campaign.

CASE DISCUSSION

This is an unusual case as there was only one objective – to secure a 'yes' vote in the forthcoming referendum on joining the European Union. Dr René Siegl of the Federation of Austrian Industrialists decided rightly that this was a case for not using advertising but to use information and persuasion to secure the desired result.

To a certain extent, they had a captive audience but only so far as the employees themselves were concerned. To persuade employees' families it was necessary to mount a really comprehensive programme of information and opportunity for serious discussion of the issues involved.

As usual, it is very difficult to isolate the effect of a particular public relations programme because of all the other influences at work, but the poll taken the day after the referendum definitely indicated that the 'Wir stimmen für Europa' campaign had a significant influence on securing the desired 'yes' vote.

Index

Index